· *Gagok*

· *Gagok*

Classical Long Lyric Song Cycle

UNESCO Intangible Cultural Heritage of Humanity Series

Publication by | Ministry of Culture, Sports and Tourism
Planning and Production by | Korean Traditional Performing Arts Foundation
Written by | Kim Young woon
Translated by | Kim Hee-sun
Photo by | Kim Sang-su

Published on December 31, 2012.

MINSOKWON Publishing Company
337-25 Daeheung-dong, Mapo-gu, Seoul, Korea

Registration: 18-1

Phone: (82-2) 804-3320 · 805-3320 · 806-3320
Fax: (82-2) 802-3346
E-mail: minsok1@chollian.net, minsok1@naver.com
Website: www.minsokwon.com

Publisher: Hong Ki-won

ISBN: 978-89-285-0379-7 93670
Price: 20,000 (won)

Printed in Korea.

Gagok

Classical Long Lyric Song Cycle

UNESCO Intangible Cultural Heritage of Humanity Series

MINSOKWON

Preface

On December 6, 2012, Arirang made it onto the UNESCO Representative List of Intangible Cultural Heritage of Humanity at the 7th UNESCO Intangible Heritage Committee held in Paris, France. With this latest decision, Korea currently holds a total of 15 cultural assets registered as UNESCO's intangible cultural heritage items, along with Jongmyo jeryeak (Jongmyo royal ancestral Confucian memorial ceremony music), Gagok (Old Korean songs), Pansori (Song and narration performed by one singer accompanied by one drummer), and Cheoyongmu (Cheoyong shaman dance).

UNESCO's Intangible Cultural Heritage of Humanity Program started in 2001 with the aim of raising awareness and encouraging protection of those items of humanity's oral and intangible heritage which are in danger of extinction. UNESCO first selected 19 original and valued oral and intangible cultural assets for its list and continues to add until now.

This book is part of the Traditional Art Text Translation Support Program run by the Ministry of Culture, Sports and Tourism of Korea. It is a translation into English of part of the series of Important Intangible Cultural Properties of Korea, published by National Research Institute of Cultural Heritage of Korea. We hope this book will provide an essential resource for those who are interested in or wish to study the Korean traditional culture but have suffered from the lack of material until now. It also provides an opportunity to communicate something of the excellence of Korean traditional culture to a wider audience.

As the old saying in Korea goes, "to inherit tradition is a way of creation (法古創新)." We have to develop along new lines, be creative and seek to move in the right direction at all times. Intangible cultural heritage is a sign of community identity which is continuously re-created in the diverse social context and plays a key role in enhancing social unity. Thus, the contents of this book form a fitting introduction to the excellence of Korean traditional culture.

Besides the UNESCO's intangible cultural heritage properties, we will endeavor to propagate a variety of Korean traditional cultural contents throughout the world.

Thank you very much.

December, 2012
Minister of Culture, Sports and Tourism
Yoo Jinryong

Preface ... *4*

General Introduction ... 8

1. *Pungnyu-bang* Music and *Gagok* ... *12*
2. *Gagok, Gasa,* and *Sijo* ... *13*

Formation and Transmission Process of *Gagok* ... 16

1. Formation of *Daeyeop*-related Pieces ... *18*
2. Formation of *Jungdaeyeop* and *Sakdaeyeop* ... *20*
3. Nineteenth-Century *Gagok* – The Formation of Today's *Gagok* ... *22*
4. Master Musicians of *Gagok* in History ... *34*
5. Poetry Anthologies and Collections of Old Notation Books ... *39*

Table of Contents

Music and Performance Practice of *Gagok* … 50

1. Structure of *Gagok* … 52
2. Rhythmic Cycles of *Gagok* … 56
3. *Gagok* Modes … 60
4. *Gagok* Vocal Style … 62
5. Performance Style of *Gagok* … 65
6. Expressions of *Gagok* … 68

Musical Characteristics of Individual Pieces and Lyrics … 70

1. *Namchang Gagok* (Male Voice) … 72
2. *Yeochang Gagok* (Female Voice) … 95

The Music-cultural Value of *Gagok* … 108

References … 117

General Introduction

General Introduction

Gagok is a vocal genre with accompaniment by a chamber ensemble of string and wind instruments. It was transmitted by aristocrats and middle–class singer/poets, called *gagaek* (guest songsters), in the *pungnyu–bang* salons or clubs during the late Joseon Dynasty. The classical vocal genres, *gagok* and *sijo*, both use the poetic form of *sijo* as lyrics, but of the two, *gagok* was developed much earlier.

Since the late Joseon Dynasty at the end of the nineteenth century, *gagok* has often been referred to by its Confucian name, *mannyeonjanghwanjigok*; prior to that, it was known as *yeongeon*, *gayo*, *gagok*, or *norae*.

Present–day *gagok* songs derive from the *sakdaeyeop* repertoire. In the early Joseon period, other types, including *mandaeyeop* and *jungdaeyeop*, as well as *sakdaeyeop*, had existed; however, in late Joseon, first *mandaeyeop*, then *jungdaeyeop* disappeared, leaving only *sakdaeyeop* remaining today. *Sakdaeyeop* has continued to develop, with the creation of pieces in four different modes: *pyeongjo*, *pyeongjo gyemyeonjo*, *ujo*, and *ujo gyemyeonjo*; only two among these–*ujo* and *ujo gyemyeonjo*–have survived since the nineteenth century. A system of gender classification was also developed and is maintained today.

Contemporary *gagok* includes 26 male and 15 female songs. A few pieces share the same title, but even these are distinct, since, even with the same title, the melodies in the male and female repertoires are different. In addition, different lyrics can be sung to the same melody; changes to the lyrics cause changes in sections of the melody, and thus it may be possible to count all individual songs with different lyrics as separate pieces. In this case, the trans-

Kim Gyeong-bae, Important Intangible Cultural Heritage Holder – Male *Gagok*

mitted *gagok* repertoires today include more than 150 pieces: the repertoire transmitted by Ha Gyu-il containing 84 male and 71 female pieces, for a total of 155; and Kim Gi-su's transcriptions numbering 100 male and 88 female songs, a total of 188 pieces.

1. *Pungnyu–bang* Music and *Gagok*

The wealthy *jungin* (middle–class) music enthusiasts of the late Joseon Dynasty gathered to enjoy musical activities by performing on instruments and singing. These music enthusiasts were called *pungnyu–gaek* (*pungnyu* guests) or *yulgaek* (literati guests), and singer/poets were known as *gagaek*.

The space where these *pungnyu–gaek* met was called *pungnyu–bang* or *yul–bang*, and the music that they enjoyed was called *pungnyu*. In pursuit of their hobby, the *pungnyu–gaek* organized associations, *akhoe* or *gye*. The most representative repertoires of *pungnyu–bang* music included *jul–pungnyu* for instrumental music, typified by the piece *Yeongsanhoesang*, and *gagok* for vocal music.

Originally, *jul–pungnyu* was performed as a chamber instrumental ensemble; the major string instruments were the *geomun–go*, *gayageum*, and *yanggeum*, while wind instruments including the *daegeum*, *sepiri*, and *danso* were added, and the *janggo* served as the only percussion instrument providing the *jangdan* rhythmic cycle. *Gagok* as vocal music was accompanied by the *julpungnyu* chamber ensemble.

Musical scores of *Mandaeyeop*, *Jungdaeyeop*, and *Sakdaeyeop*–the prototypes of *gagok*–and for *Yeongsanhoesang*–related pieces were found among old scores documenting the music of the *pungnyu–bang*. It can thus be conjectured that the instrumental version of *Yeongsanhoesang* and vocal *gagok* had been established as the major repertoires of *pungnyu–bang* music from earlier periods.

2. *Gagok, Gasa,* and *Sijo*

The most representative genres of literature written in Korean during the late Joseon period are the poetic forms *gasa* and *sijo*. Unlike *gasa*, with its long lyric form, the short, regular poetic form of *sijo* has been used in lyrics for *mandaeyeop*, *jungdaeyeop* and *sakdaeyeop* from earlier periods. For example, *Dansimga* (Song of Thoughtful Mind Never Changes), written by *po–eun* (pen name) Jeong Mong–ju, was used as the lyrics for a *jungdaeyeop* found in the *Yanggeumsinbo* score. Since it used a *sijo* poem from the literati, the *gagok* can be distinguished from *minyo*, folk songs, and *japga*, professional folk songs.

The three genres, *gagok*, *gasa*, and *sijo*, are often collectively referred to as *jeongga*, (lit. "Righteous Music") but *gasa*, the long lyric poem with irregular strophic form, can be quite distinct from *gagok* and *sijo*. The latter two are similar, since each uses *sijo* poems for its lyrics, but, there too, form, instrumental accompaniment, and repertoire differ between them. *Sijo* is less professional in terms of music and appeared much later than *gagok*. Thus, of the two musical genres, *gagok* is considered as the music of professionals, while *sijo* is viewed as the genre of amateur music enthusiasts.

Gagok is the most representative vocal genre of the literati of the late Joseon period. It diversified and evolved to form various repertoires, and gave birth to many masterpieces of *sijo* poetry.

Jo Sun-ja, Important Intangible Cultural Heritage Holder – Female *Gagok*

和道力

Formation and Transmission Process of *Gagok*

Formation and Transmission Process of *Gagok*

1. Formation of *Daeyeop*–related Pieces

The current genre name, *gagok*, stems from *Gagokwollyu* (The Mainstream of *Gagok*), song collections of *gagok* complied in 1876. These songs were called *yeongeon* or *gayo* in other, earlier collections, e.g., *Cheongguyeongoen* and *Haedonggayo*.

The prototypes of *gagok* were *daeyeop*–related pieces, such as *Mandaeyeop*, *Jungdaeyeop*, and *Sakdaeyeop*. The first score to include *daeyeop*–related pieces was *Geumhapjabo* (1572), which contained a *geomun–go* score for *mandaeyeop*. According to notes in the score, *mandaeyeop* is in *pyeongjo* mode, and consists of five sections (as in the following) and a postlude. The text is as follows.

<Text of *Pyeongjo Mandayeop* in *Geumhapjabo*>

① Onarina onarina / ② maeileonarina

③ Jeommudido saedido onari / ④ saerina

⑤ Maeildhangshangui onari oshosheo [postlude]

In *Yanggeumsinbo*, compiled in 1610, both *mandaeyeop* and four pieces of *jungdaeyeop* are found, but no *sakdaeyeop* is included. However, it can be conjectured that *sakdaeyeop* had also existed, since references to it appear in an annotation of the score, which states that "*sakdaeyeop* is used in dance accompaniment,...should not be preferred for the *geomun–go*." The preface to the score speaks to the formation of *daeyeop*–related pieces. The author writes, "Currently–performed *mandaeyeop*, *jungdaeyeop*, and *sakdaeyeop* all originated from *Gwajeong Samgigok*. *Gwajeong* is a nickname of Jeong Seo." That is, three *daeyeop*–related pieces performed during the early seventeenth century all descended from *Gwajeong Samgigok* by Jeong Seo, a Goryeo literati–officer. *Gwajeong Samgigok* refers to *Jinjak*, from the collection of scores, *Daeakhubo*. The piece consists of three main sections. The first section is made up of five sub–sections of *jeonggang*, *junggang*, *hugang*, *buyeop*, and *daeyeoeum*. The second section consists of three sub–sections of *daeyeop*, *buyeop*, and *daeyeoeum*. The third section contains six sub–sections of *yiyeop*, *samyeop*, *sayeop*, *buyeop*, *oyeop*, and *daeyeoeum*. Writings in the preface of *Yanggeumsinbo* indicate the relationship between the *daeyeop* sections of the piece and the *daeyeop*–related pieces.

As indicated earlier, four *jungdaeyeop* pieces are included in *Yanggeumsinbo*. The second lyric of one of the pieces, *Pyeongjo Jungdaeyeop*, was the *Dansimga* of Poeun Jeong Mong–ju. The structure of this song is as follows.

<Text of *Pyeongjo Jungdaeyeop* in *Yanggeumsinbo*>

① Imomi jugeojugeo / ② ilbaekbeon goteo jugeo

③ Baekgori jintoidoeyeo neoksirado itgo oebgo /

④ nimhyanghan

⑤ Ilpyeondansimiya gasiljuri isirya [postlude]

The division of the three–section poems into five sections, and the existence of a postlude are the same in current *gagok*. While the *mandaeyeop* in *Geumhapjabo* and *Yanggeumsinbo* were only in *pyeongjo* mode, the *Jungdaeyeop* in *Yanggeumsinbo* occurred in four different modes: *pyeongjo, pyeongjo gyemyeonjo, ujo,* and *ujo gyemyeonjo*. *Mandaeyeop* is no longer sung or performed in instrumental form, and has disappeared because the music was in a very slow tempo.

2. Formation of *Jungdaeyeop* and *Sakdaeyeop*

In later scores, the number of pieces in each mode of *Jungdaeyeop* have increased. Those pieces were entitled *Jungdaeyeop, Jeil,* and *Jei* in different scores, and were often written as works of *Chojungdaeyeop, Ijungdaeyeop,* and *Samjungdaeyeop*. By the late seventeenth century, *Jungdaeyeop* completely adopted the three–part structure in individual mode, appearing in several scores including *Yeondaesojanggeumbo, Unmonggeumbo* (1707), and *Hangeumsinbo* (1724). Close examination of these scores shows that the introductions of three pieces belonging to the same mode start in different ways, some beginning high and some low.

Jungdaeyeop evolved and developed in several modes and various pieces until the eighteenth century, but by the early nineteenth century, only one piece with four different modes was to be found in *Yuyeji, pyeongjo* and *pyeongjo gyemyeonjo. Jungdaeyeop* had disappeared, and only *ujo* and *ujo gyemyeonjo Jungdaeyeop* are found in the score *Samjukgeumbo* (1841).

Sakdaeyeop was not included in *Yanggeumsinbo* (1610), but was performed along with *Jungdaeyeop* during that period, as described earlier. Various *Sakdaeyeop* scores were also found in *Hyeongeumdongmunryugi* (1620). *Sakdaeyeop* had evolved into four pieces in different modes: two pieces in *pyeongjo* and *ujo* modes, and one piece each in *pyeongjo gyemyeonjo* and *ujo gyemyeonjo,* as appeared in *Jeungbogogeumbo.* Three pieces in four modes of *Sakdaeyeop* appeared in *Sinjeunggeumbo* (1680). Again, three pieces in *pyeongjo* and *pyeongjo gyemyeonjo,* and three pieces in *ujo* and *ujo gyemyeonjo* appeared in *Hangeumsinbo* (1724). These songs also differed in their beginning melodies between high and low.

<Table 1> *Jungdaeyeop, Bukjeon, Sakdaeyeop* in *Hangeumsinbo*

Modes	*Pyeongjo*	*Ujo*	*Pyeongjo Gyemyeonjo*	*Ujo Gyemyeonjo*
Pieces	*Ujo Jungdaeyeop 1*	*Ujo Jungdaeyeop 1*	*Ujo*	*Ujo Gyemyeonjo Jungdaeyeop 1*
	Pyeongjo Jungdaeyeop 2	*Ujo Jungdaeyeop 2*	*Gyemyeonjo Jungdaeyeop 1*	*Ujo Gyemyeonjo Jungdaeyeop 2*
	Pyeongjo Jungdaeyeop 3	*Ujo Jungdaeyeop 3*	*Ujo Gyemyeonjo Jungdaeyeop 2*	*Ujo Gyemyeonjo Jungdaeyeop 3*
	Pyeongjo Jungdaeyeop 1	*Ujo Bukjeon 1*	*Ujo Gyemyeonjo Jungdaeyeop 3*	*Ujo Gyemyeonjo Bukjeon 1*
	Pyeongjo Bukjeon 2	*Ujo Bukjeon 2*	*Ujo Gyemyeonjo Bukjeon 1*	*Ujo Gyemyeonjo Bukjeon 2*
	Pyeongjo Sakdaeyeop 1	*Ujo Sakdaeyeop 1*	*Ujo Gyemyeonjo Bukjeon 2 Ujo*	*Ujo Gyemyeonjo Sakdaeyeop 1*
	Pyeongjo Sakdaeyeop 2	*Ujo Sakdaeyeop 2*	*Gyemyeonjo Sakdaeyeop 1*	*Ujo Gyemyeonjo Sakdaeyeop 2*
	Pyeongjo Sakdaeyeop 3	*Ujo Sakdaeyeop 3*	*Ujo Gyemyeonjo Sakdaeyeop 2*	*Ujo Gyemyeonjo Sakdaeyeop 3*
		Ujo Sakdaeyeop 4	*Ujo Gyemyeonjo Sakdaeyeop 3*	*Ujo Gyemyeonjo Sakdaeyeop 4*

The most important change in *Jungdaeyeop* and *Sakdaeyeop* during this period was the establishment of high-register style. When the pieces in *pyeongjo* and *pyeonjo gyemyeonjo* were no longer sung, only *ujo* and *ujo gyemyeonjo gagok* remained. As a result, *Mandaeyeop* among *Mandaeyeop, Jungdaeyeop* and *Sakdaeyeop* were no longer performed in the early eighteenth century, and *Jungdaeyeop* also disappeared during the early nineteenth century. Later, as *Sakdaeyeop* continued to evolve, it became the *gagok* song cycle of the late nineteenth century, transmitted to the present.

3. Nineteenth-Century *Gagok* – The Formation of Today's *Gagok*

Both *Jungdaeyeop* and *Sakdaeyeop* were performed by the singer-poets in earlier periods. Since the nineteenth century, however, *Jungdaeyeop* has rarely been sung and only *Sakdaeyeop* has remained as the major *gagok* repertoire. Furthermore, *pungnyu* guests favored *gagok* in *ujo* and *pyeongjo gyemyeonjo* modes, with their higher–register style, over *pyeongjo* and *pyeongjo gyemyeonjo* modes with their low–register style. This led to the popularization of *Sakdaeyeop* in *ujo* and *ujo gyemyeonjo* modes. At the same time, new derivation of *gagok*, including *nong*, *nak*, and *pyeon* styles, have evolved. Also repertoires for female voice have appeared. The extension of repertoires and the establishment of both male and female repertoires enabled the development of the *gagok* song cycle. Also, *banu bangye* (half *ujo* and half *gyemyeon* mode, from *ujo* to *gyemyeonjo* or *gyemyeonjo* to *ujo*) was created for the purpose of modulation.

Kim Yeong-gi, Important Intangible Cultural Heritage Holder – Female *Gagok*

In addition, *gagok* was performed at court banquets, using text for the court *jeongjae* dance, *jeongjae changsa,* sung to *gagok* melodies. This also encouraged the expansion of *gagok* repertoires and the invigoration of *gagok* for female voice. Further, it helped to establish the current *sagwanpungnyu* (wind ensemble) instrumental tradition, since *jeongjae changsa* was accompanied by a wind ensemble.

1) Appearance of *Nong, Nak,* and *Pyeon*

The repertoires of *Nongyeop, Gyerak,* and *Pyeonsakdaeyeop* were compiled in *Yuyeji,* an early nineteenth–century *pungnyu* music manuscript. It writes that *nong* "grooves with wide vibrato," *nak* indicates "cheerful melody like spring flowers in full bloom," or "comparatively tranquil compared to grooving *nong,* yet waving like flowing water." *Pyeon* denotes *yeokkeum* (series) or *saseol* (longer text), using ten–beat condensed rhythmic cycle rather than sixteen–beat regular rhythm in *gagok.*

Among *nong*–style pieces, the first, *Eollong,* is found in *Samjukgeumbo* (1841), while *Pyeollong* originally appears in *Hyeongeumoeumtongron* (1886), and the first *Urong* in *Bangsanhanssigeumbo* (1916). From the repertoire of *nak*–style pieces, *Gyerak* and *Urak* first appeared in *Yuyeji; Gyemyeonsaksijo, Ujonaksijo,* and *Eollaksijo* in *Gangeoigeumbo;* and *Eollak* and *Pyeollak* in *Samjukgeumbo.* Thus, it can be said that four current major pieces of *nak*–style *gagok–Gyerak, Urak, Eollak,* and *Pyeollak*–were established in the mid–nineteenth century. This means that the *nak* style was formed earlier than the other styles of *nong* and *pyeon*.

Pyeon–style works basically sing *saseol sijo* (prose–style *sijo* poetry); early *saseol sijo gagok* appeared in the *gagok* anthology *Manhwaengcheongnyu* in *Jinbon Cheongguyeongeon* (1728). However, *saseol sijo gagok* were not to be found in the old manuscript *Nangongsinbo* (1728) or other eighteenth–century manuscripts. The first *pyeon*–style piece, *Pyeonsakdaeyeop*, was recorded in *Yuyeji*, followed by *Pyeonsakdaeyeop* and *Pyeollak* in *Samjukgeumbo* (1841). *Eonpyeon* first appeared in *Huiyu* (ca. late nineteenth century) with *Upyeon* in *Bangsanhanssigeumbo* (1916). Thus, it can be said that the current ten–beat *pyeon*–style *gagok* was established in the early twentieth century when *Bangsanhanssigeumbo* (1916) was compiled.

While most *gagok* texts until the eighteenth century were *pyeong sijo* (regular *sijo* poetry) with approximately forty-five syllables, nineteenth–century *nong*– and *nak*–style *so*–*gagok* songs used *eot sijo* (irregular *sijo*) with extended second or third lines. *Pyeon* employs *saseol sijo*, which reflects the flexible forms and expressions of *sijo* literature, and this has also influenced the musical tradition.

2) *Soyong, Junggeo, Pyeonggeo,* and *Dugeo*

Early *Sakdaeyeop* in the four different modes: *pyeongjo, pyeongjo gyemyeonjo, ujo,* and *ujo gyemyeonjo*, evolved into *Sakdaeyeop, Jeil, Jei,* and *Jesam*, respectively, and were also called by different names–*Chosakdaeyeop, Isakdaeyeop,* and *Samsakdaeyeop*–according to different manuscripts. *Jesa* appeared in *ujo* and *ujo gyemyeonjo* in *Hangeumsinbo* (1724), and in *pyeongjo* and *pyeongjo gyemyeonjo* in *Nangongsinbo* (1728). All of these songs begin in a different low or high register.

During the late nineteenth century, few pieces were derived from pieces beginning in a low register, and *Junggeo, Pyeonggeo,* and *Dugeo* were variation beginning in a low or high register. The word *geo* in the names of these pieces, which first appeared in *Hyeongeumoeumtongron* (1886), means "to raise" in the beginning or middle part of the song. *Junggeo* (lit., raise in the middle) rises "after 12 beats of the first prose" based on the melody of *Isakdaeyeop; Pyeonggeo* (lit., raise in plain) begins in the middle register, not high or low compared to *Isakdaeyeop;* and *Dugeo* (lit., raise the head) begins in a high register. However, a few *Sakdaeyeop* variations were found in earlier manuscripts, including *joim* in *Samjukgeumbo* and *Joimdaeyeop* in *Huiyu. Joim* in these pieces means "to tighten up"; musically, this means to sing in fast tempo, and scholars agree that *joim* is the same as *Dugeo. Sosakdaeyeop* in *Bangsanhanssigeumbo* is generally interpreted as *Dugeo.*

Prior to the nineteenth century, *Samdakdaeyeop, Soi,* and *Soyong* were followed by *Joim,* and were compiled in *Samjukgeumbo* (1841); however, *Soi* was a separate piece from *Samsakdaeyeop, Joim,* and *Soyong. Samsakdaeyeop* is set in a high register only for the first prose section, while *Soyong* is sung entirely in a high register. *Dugeo* is also sung in a high register at the beginning like *Samsakdaeyeop;* however, the degree of its "rise" is different, and *Soyong* is a variation of *Samsakdaeyeop.*

Variations of *Isakdaeyeop,* including *Junggeo, Pyeonggeo,* and *Dugeo,* appeared in the late nineteenth century, and variations of *Samsakdaeyeop*, like *Soyong*, date from the early nineteenth century. In addition, few piece names were found, including *Dansakdaeyeop* in *Ilsageumbo* (1884) and *Yeokyangaun* and *Saksakdaeyeop* in *Uheongeumbo*. This indicates that a few derived pieces were established during the developmental period of *gagok* but were not transmitted.

Kim Gyeong-bae, Important Intangible Cultural Heritage Holder – Male *Gagok*

3) Formation of Male and Female Voice and an Alternative Singing Style

Unlike current *gagok*, gender–based repertoires were not found in early *daeyeop*–related *gagok*. It can be said that there were no separate repertoires for male and female voices when *gagok* was called *Mandaeyeop, Jungdaeyeop,* and *Sakdaeyeop*.

The first *gagok* piece for female voice was found in *Samjukgeumbo* (1841), which also documents the first and only surviving male and female *gagok* duet. The piece is known today as *Taepyeongga;* it was named *Cheongseong-sakdaeyeop* in *Samjukgeumbo,* and the title *Taepyeongga* was first used in *Hyeo-ngeumoeumtongron* (1886). *Hwangyerak,* the song sung only by females in the current *gagok* repertoire, first appeared in *Seogeumgagok* (1884).

The early form of alternating male and female style and song–cycle structure ending with *Taepyeongga* was found in *Samjukgeumbo* (1841) and *Hyeonhakgeumbo* (1852). *Ujo Isakdaeyeop, Ujo Jorim,* and *Gyemyeon Jorim* were female songs and *Cheongseongsakdaeyeop* in *Samjukgeumbo* was a male and female duet. *Isakdaeyeop (gi-i), Isakdaeyeop (gi-sa),* and *Samsakdaeyeop* in *ujo* mode, and *Isakdaeyeop (gi-i), Isakdaeyeop (gi-sa),* and *Isakdaeyeop (gi-o)* in *gyemyeonjo Hyeonakgeumbo* were for female voice and this piece was compiled along with male voice alternatively.

Thus, the alternating male–female singing style began during the mid–nineteenth century and was firmly established by the late nineteenth century, as documented by the appearance of *Taepyeongga, Hwangyerak,* and other pieces in *Hyeongeumoeumtongron* (1886), *Hwigeumgagokbo* (1893), and *Gagokwollyu* (1876).

When *gagok* was established as a song–cycle, pieces in *ujo* and *gyemyeonjo* modes were performed as a series, and pieces for modulation between modes–*banu bangye*–also appeared. For example, *Banyeop* was needed as a bridge from *Ujo Soyong* to *Gyemyeon Chosakdaeyeop*; *Pyeollak* served a similar function as transition between *Eollak* and *Pyeonsakdaeyeop*, as did *Hwangyerak* between *Urak* and *Gyerak*. The alternating male–female singing style and the song–cycle with different modes were firmly established in the late nineteenth century and led to the heyday of *gagok* to come.

Table 2 illustrates the diversification and development of *gagok*, from sixteenth–and seventeenth–century *daeyeop*–related pieces to the current *gagok* song–cycle.

<Table 2> Diversification and Development of *Gagok* Repertoires

Before Mid 17C	Mid 17C – Mid 18C	Late 18C – Early 19C	Mid 19C	Late 19C	Early 20C	Current
Ujo Sakdaeyeop	*Ujo Chosakdaeyeop*	*Uchoyeop*	*Chosakdaeyeop*	*Chosakdaeyeop*	*Chosakdaeyeop*	*Chosakdaeyeop*
	Ujo Isakdaeyeop	*Uiyeop*	*Isakdaeyeop*	*Isakdaeyeop*	*Isakdaeyeop*	*Isakdaeyeop*
				Junggeo	*Geojungseong*	*Junggeo*
				Pyeonggeo	*Pyeongseong*	*Pyeonggeo*
				Dugeo	*Sosakdaeyeop*	*Dugeo*
			Joim			
	Ujo Samsakdaeyeop	*Usamyeop*	*Samsakdaeyeop*	*Samsakdaeyeop*	*Samsakdaeyeop*	*Samsakdaeyeop*
			Soi	–	*Sorsetchi*	

<Table 2> Diversification and Development of *Gagok* Repertoires

Before Mid 17C	Mid 17C – Mid 18C	Late 18C – Early 19C	Mid 19C	Late 19C	Early 20C	Current
			Soyong	*Soyongi*	*Soyongi*	*Soyong*
			Banyeop	*Yuldang*	*Banyeopdaeyeop*	*Banyeop*
Gyemyeonjo Sakdaeyeop	*Gyemyeonjo Sakdaeyeop*	*Gyechoyeop*	*Chosakdaeyeop*	*Chosakdaeyeop*	*Chosakdaeyeop*	*Chosakdaeyeop*
	Gyemyeonjo Isakdaeyeop	*Gyeiyeop*	*Isakdaeyeop*	*Isakdaeyeop*	*Isakdaeyeop*	*Isakdaeyeop*
				Junggeo	*Geojungseong*	*Junggeo*
				Pyeonggeo	*Pyeonggeo*	*Pyeonggeo*
				Dugeo	*Sosakdaeyeop*	*Dugeo*
			Joim			
	Gyemyeonjo Samsakdaeyeop	*Gyesamyeop*	*Samsakdaeyeop*	*Samsakdaeyeop*	*Samsakdaeyeop*	*Samsakdaeyeop*
			Soi	–	*Soisetchi*	
			Soyong	–	*Soyongi*	*Soyong*
		Nongyeop	*Nong*	*Pyeollong*	*Gyerong*	*Pyeongrong*
			Eotlong	*Eollong*	*Eollong / Manheong*	*Eollong*
			Urong	*Uyuldang*	*Urong*	*Urong*
		Urak	*Ujo Naksijo*	*Urak*	*Urak*	*Urak*
				Hwangyerak	*Hwangyerak*	*Hwangyerak*
		Gyerak	*Gyerak*	*Gyerak*	*Gyerak*	*Gyerak*
		Eollaksijo	*Eollak*	*Eollak*	*Eollak*	*Eollak*
			Pyeollak	*Pyeollak*	*Pyeollak*	*Pyeollak*
		Pyeonsakdaeyeop	*Pyeonsakdaeyeop*	*Pyeon*	*Gyepyeon*	*Pyeonsakdaeyeop*
			Eonpyeon	–	*Eonpyeon*	*Eonpyeon*
					Upyeon	*Upyeon*
			Cheongseong sakdaeyeop	*Taepyeongga*	*Gyemyeon Taepyeongga*	*Taepyeongga*

4) *Gagok* Performance in Court

Gaja (professional *gagok* singers) and *gachabi yeoryeong* (female *gagok* singers) have performed at court banquets, like *jinchan* and *jinyeon*, since the early nineteenth century, around the time of King Sunjo. As middle–class *gagok* singers, *gaja* have performed *gagok* in *oeyeon* (banquets for royal male members and royal subjects), while female singers performed in *naeyeon* (banquets for royal female members) and *yayeon* (The night banquet). Both sung *gagok* with texts called *akga* or *ga*, accompanied by *sechwi* (chamber band) ensembles. The text of *Taepyeongga* was also included in *Jeongjaemudoholgi* (Protocol of Court Dance), and thus, it can be conjectured that court musicians

Instrumental Accompaniment for *Gagok*

(*akgong*) and female court dancers (*yeoryeong*) might have sung *gagok* at the end of court banquets as a blessing.

The most important role of *gagok* was found in *jeongjae changsa* (singing with court dance). *Jeongjae* sung with sino–Korean and pure Korean *changsa* texts were *Bongnaeui, Gyeongpungdo, Mansumu, Saseonmu, Muaemu,* and *Yukhwadae.* Among these, *Gyeongpungdo, Mansumu, Saseonmu,* and *Muaemu* were sung with *gagok pyeon* melodies, while *Bongnaeui* and *Yukhwadae* were sung with *nong, gyerak,* and *pyeon* repertoires. Another court *jeongjae, Hyangryeongmu,* was accompanied by three *gagok Gyerak,* one each of *changsa, chileonjeolgu* (seven–syllable prose), and *chileonyulsi* (seven–syllable poetry). The court *jeongjae changsa* repertoires of the late Joseon have been transmitted down to the present. The *Bongnaeui* text "*ppurikipeun…*" (Deep roots…) is preserved in *Pyeongrong* for male voice, while another *Bongnaeui* text, "*juguk taewang*" (King of Chu Dynasty…) and the *Hyangryeongmu* texts "*Okjeonyogung…*" (Jade Palace…) and "*Hwaranyoji…*" (Flowers in full bloom…) survive in *Gyerak.* The *Mansumu* text "*ojeomanjae…*" is also found in *Pyeonsudaeyeop,* and the *Bongnaeui* text "*bulgeunsae…*" (red bird…) is found in *Pyeonsudaeyeop* for female voice. Even though it cannot be ascertained whether it was used in the late Joseon period, the current *Eollak* contains the text of *Cheoyongmu*: "*Sillaseongdae…*" (Glory of Silla…); and the text of *Bonghwangeum*: "*Sanhacheolliguk…*" is maintained in *Upyeon.* These *gagok,* performed at court banquets in the late Joseon era, were *nong, nak* and *pyeon* pieces, since their cheerful and upbeat feelings suited the banquet atmosphere.

At the same time, these pieces accommodated extended text more eas-

Jo Sun-ja, Important Intangible Cultural Heritage Holder – Female *Gagok*

ily than regular *sijo*, and were fast in tempo, and thus were proper to perform at the end of *jeongjae*. Three pieces from the *nong*, *nak*, and *pyeon* repertoires are the most important in current performance practice and serve as the basis for *Jajinhanip*, the instrumentalized version of *gagok*, which is the most widely performed in ensemble, duet, and solo formats. The musical excellence of these pieces possibly made pieces were employed in court banquets since the mid–nineteenth century.

The first *gagok* performance by *gachabi yeoryeong* in a court banquet was in 1829 (the twenty–ninth year of King Sunjo's reign), which preceded the first appearance of female vocal repertoire in the manuscript *Samjukgeumbo* (1841). The mid–nineteenth century was a time of flourishing for female vocal *gagok* and the active participation of *gachabi yeoryeong* in court banquets. Thus, it can be argued that *gagok* performance by female musicians of the court became the basis for the development of female *gagok* performance.

4 . Master Musicians of *Gagok* in History

The main figures of *gagok* culture during the late Joseon period were *jungin*, *gagaek* singers of middle–class origins, who developed friendships with other *pungnyugaek* and organized *gadan* song societies or *yulgye* urban associations. The most representative *gagaek* were Kim Cheon-taek, Kim Su-jang, and Pak Hyo-gwan. More recently, the singer Ha Gyu-il contributed to the transmission of *gagok* in the modern period.

• **Kim Cheon-taek** 김천택(金天澤)

Sijo poet and singer–poet during the reigns of kings Sunjong and Yeonjo under pen name *Nampa* 남파 (南坡), Kim was a *yeohang* (urban middle–class professionals, administrators, and merchants) *gagaek* and a provincial government officer during King Sukjong's reign. He compiled the *gagok* anthology *Cheongguyeongeon*, with *sijo* classical poetry sung in *gagok* form. Noted as "excellent in music as well as literature" by Jeong Yun–gyeong in the preface to the anthology, Kim was the leading figure of *gagok* society. He enjoyed the companionship of the other *gagaek* Kim Yu–gi, Kim Seong-gi, and Kim Jung-ryeo, and associated with the *Gyeongjeong-sangadan* (*Gyeongjeongsan Gagok* Society). He left about eighty *sijo* poems in *Cheong-*

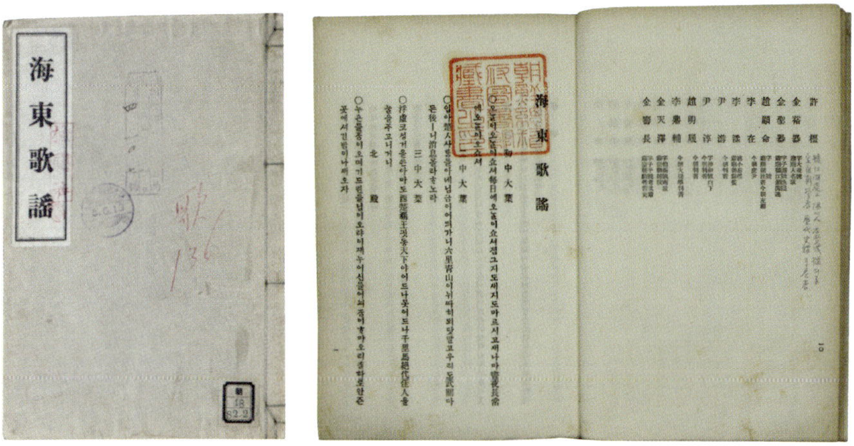

Names of Kim Cheon-taek and Kim Su-jang in "Gogeumchanggajessi," the preface to *Haedonggayo*

guyeongeon and *Haedonggayo*.

• **Kim Su-jang** 김수장(金壽長)

Born in 1690, the *gagaek* of the late Joseon era, with pen name *Nogajae* 노가재(老歌齋), Kim compiled the *gagok* anthology *Haedonggayo*. He built the house called *nogajae* 노가재(老歌齋) in Seoul Hwagaedong, and led the *nogajaegadan* (*Nogajae Gag-ok* Society) and *gagok* activities. As a poet himself, he wrote about 130 *sijo* poems. These include thirty-nine *saseol sijo* which describe the affection between men and women, and the lifestyles and emotions of middle–class people.

• **Jang U-byeok** 장우벽(張友璧, 1735–1809)

Seoul–born *gagaek* during the reigns of King Yeongjo and King Jeongjo, Jang was a local governmental officer at Tongryewon, the office of rites in the Joseon

Dynasty, but resigned after one year. He was known to sing *gagok* well and developed his own vocal style as a result of research, often in uncertain sources; he was referred to as the initiator of the *maehwaejeom jangdan* (sixteen beat *jangdan* pattern) in *gagok*. His vocal style was transmitted to the later generations of *gagaek* including O Dong-rae, Jeong Jung-bo, Choe Su-bo, Ha Jun-gwon, Ha Gyu-il, Pak Hyo-gwan, Hong Jin-won, and Chu Gyo-sun.

• **O Dong-rae** 오동래(吳東萊)

A *gagaek* in the time of kings Heonjong and Cheoljong in the Joseon period, he learned *gagok* from Jang U-byeok and taught it to his disciples, including Jeong Jung-bo, Choe Su-bo, and Pak Hyo-gwan. Only Choe Su-bo's version has been preserved today.

• **Ha Jun-gwon** 하준권(河俊權)

A Seoul–born *gagaek* during the late Joseon period, whose name was sometimes given as Ha Jung-gon. He was the leading *gagaek* along with Pak Hyo-gwan. A disciple of Choe Su-bo, he also influenced his nephew and master singer of the modern period, Ha Gyu-il.

• **Choe Su-bo** 최수보(崔守甫)

A *gagaek* during King Gojong's reign. As a disciple of O Dong-rae, Choe was the leading *gagaek* along with Pak Hyo-gwan. His *gagok* repertoire was transmitted through his disciple, Ha Jun-gwon, to Ha Gyu-il.

• **Pak Hyo-gwan** 박효관(朴孝寬)

A *gagaek* during King Gojong's reign, with pen name *Unae* 운애 (雲崖), his birth and death dates are not known. He learned Jang U-byeok's *gagok* repertoire from O Dong-rae. Pak compiled one of the three major *gagok* anthologies, *Gagokwollyu*, with his disciple An Min-yeong. He was especially beloved by Daewongun (King Gojong's father), who gave him his pen name. He also led *noingye* and *seungpyeonggye gagok* societies. He left thirteen *sijo* poems in *Gagokwollyu*.

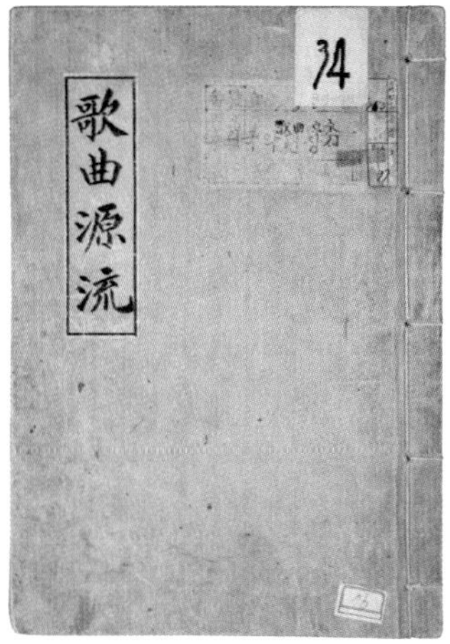

Gagokwollyu

• **An Min-yeong** 안민영(安玟英)

A *gagaek* during the reign of King Gojong with pen name *Juong* 주옹 (周翁), An's birth and death dates are not known. He belonged to the *seoeol* (born to the aristocracy but by a concubine) class. With his teacher Pak Hyo-gwan, he compiled *Gagokwollyu*. He also compiled his own personal poetry anthology, *Geumokchongbu*, and left twenty-six *sijo* poems in *Gagokwollyu* and about 180 poems in *Geumokchongbu*.

• **Ha Sun-il** 하순일(河順一)

A Seoul-born *gagaek* during the late Joseon period, he is also known by the names Cheong-il and Jeong-il. Ha was a former governor of Goseong county in

Gyeongsangnamdo Province. He learned *gagok* from Pak Hyo-gwan and became well–known as a *gagok* singer. He was also famous for his *geomun–go* (six–stringed fretted zither) performance. He taught *gagok* for male and female voice at *Joseonjeon-gakjeonseupso* (Joseon Music Institute) and was one of the initiators of *Joyanggurakbu* (Joyang Club), the first private music institute in Korea.

• **Ha Gyu-il** 하규일(河圭一, 1867–1937)

The most famous *gagok* master of modern times, with the pen name *Geumha* 금하 (琴下), Ha was born in Seoul and was a cousin of another *gagok* master, Ha Sun-il. Ha learned *gagok* from his uncle, Ha Jung-gon, and Ha's teacher, Choe Su-bo, and became the most famous *gagok* master. He served as a judge at Hanseong (former name of Seoul) courthouse and governor of Jinan County, as well as other government positions. He also served as a principal of *Joseonjeongakjeonseupso.* In-stitute in 1911, and headmaster for the *yeoak* class of *Joseonjeongakjeonseupso* in 1912. He established *Daejeonggwonbeon* (Daejeong Female Entertainers Association) in 1912 and *Joseongwonbeon* (Joseon Female Entertainers Association) in 1924. He also taught *gagok*, *gasa*, and *sijo* to students at *Yiwangjikaakbu* (Royal Music Institute). He compiled a *gagok* anthology, *Gainpilhyu*, in 1931. Currently, eighty-nine male and seventy-one female *gagok* pieces, as well as eight *gasa* (narrative songs) and *sijo* (sung short poems) have been transmitted from Ha.

Figure 1 shows the lineage of modern *gagok* transmission, from Jang U-byeok to Yi Byeong-seong and Yi Ju-hwan.

<Figure 1> Lineage of *Gagok* Transmission

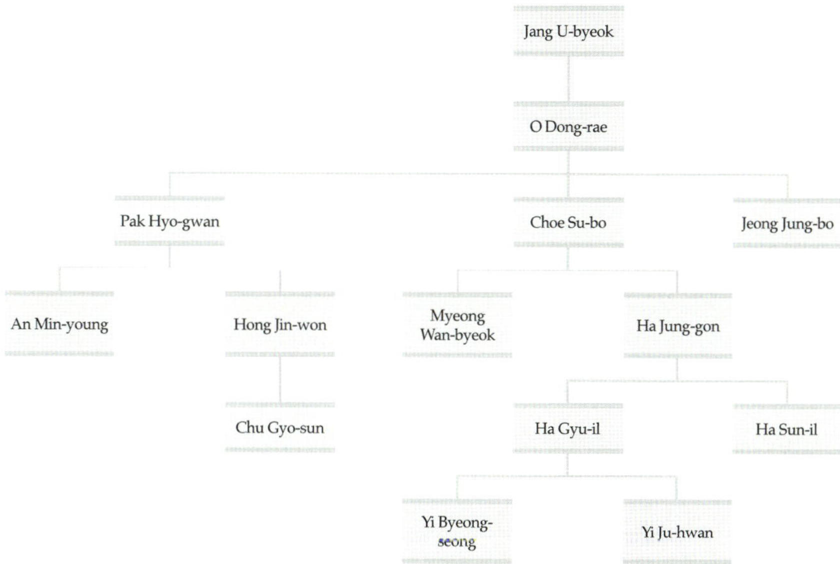

5. Poetry Anthologies and Collections of Old Notation Books

Several written sources on *gagok* exist, including compilations of *gagok* texts, old notation books documenting the music accompanying *gagok*, and music scores containing notation of *gagok* melodies. Besides the three major *gagok* anthologies–*Cheongguyeongeon*, *Haedonggayo*, and *Gagokwollyu*–other anthologies, including *Donggaseon*, *Daedongpunga*, *Gaekakbo*, *Byeongwagagokjip*,

Gogeumgagok, and *Namhuntaepyeongga*, have survived.

Gagok manuscripts include the anthologies *Gagokwollyu*, *Hyeopyul-daeseong*, and *Yeochanggayorok*, which employ *yeoneumpyo* neumatic notation, using a variety of simple symbols to denote vocal techniques and the basic direction of the melody, and a few other manuscripts and notation books, like *Hyeonhakgeumbo* and *Hakpogeumbo*, which records *Jungdaeyeop* with melody–line notation.

The majority of old notation books for *gagok* instrumental accompaniment are *geomun–go* scores and a number of *yanggeum* (dulcimer) notation books which have survived. Others exist, including books of notation for *bipa*, *hwigeum*, and *gayageum*, but no notation collections for wind instruments has been found. Only scores for *so* (pan flute) and *saenghwang* (mouth organ) have been found, in *Baekunamgeumbo* and *Yuyeji*, respectively.

Cheongguyeongeon

· ***Cheongguyeongeon*** 청구영언(青丘永言)

This *gagok* anthology, complied by Kim Cheon-taek in 1728 (fourth year of the reign of King Yeongjo) consists of a one volume manuscript. It is considered to be one of the three most important *gagok* anthologies, along with *Haedonggayo* and *Gagokwollyu*. *Cheonggu* in the book title refers to Korea, and *yeongeon* refers to songs. Alternate versions use different Chinese characters like 青丘詠言 and 青邱永言. Until today, seven versions have been

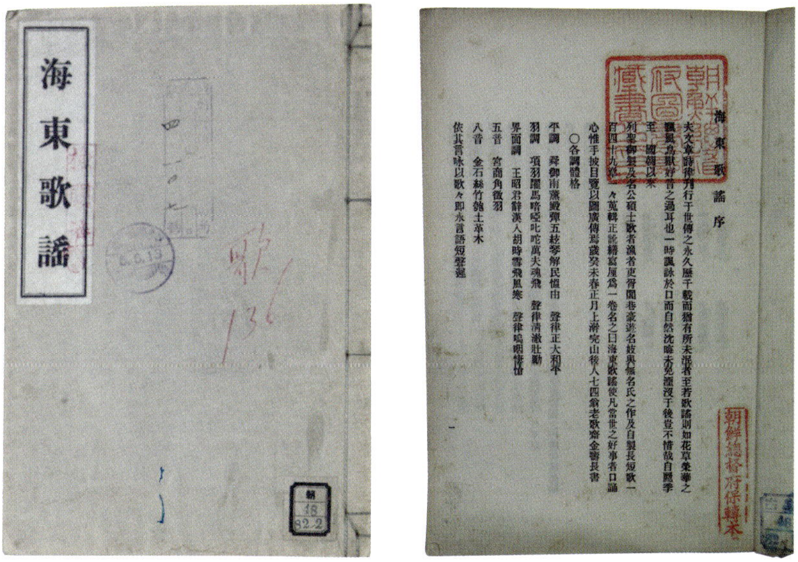

Haedonggayo

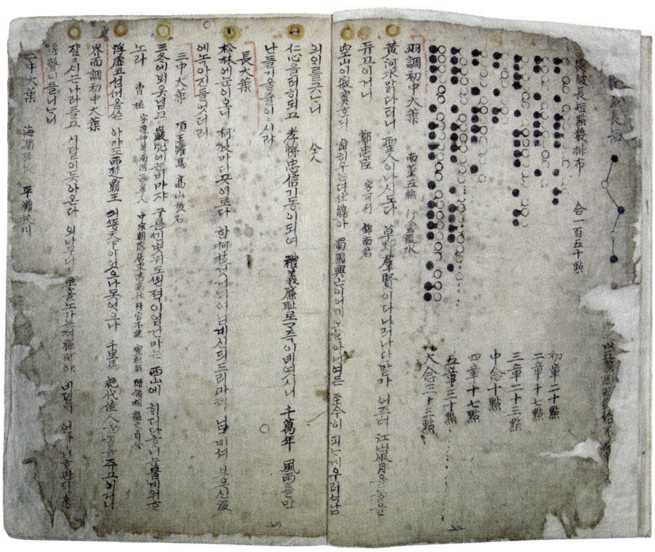

Janggo Jangdan in *Gagokwollyu*

found, and one authenticated book is called *Jinbon Cheongguyeongeon* (A genuine *Cheongguyeongeon*). *Jinbon Cheongguyeongeon* contains a total of 580 poems, divided between the sections *Chojungdaeyeop, Ijungdaeyeop, Samjungdaeyeop, Bukjeon, Ibukjeon, Chosakdaeyeop, Isakdaeyeop, Samsakdaeyeop*, and *Naksijo*. Among these, the *Isakdaeyeop* section is subdivided into masterpieces of the Goryeo and Joseon periods, *Yeolseongeoje, Yeohangyukin* (six urban middle-class poets), *Gyususamin* (three female poets), *Yeondaegyeolgo*, and *Mumyeongssi* (unknown authors).

· *Haedonggayo* 해동가요 (海東歌謠)

Several alternate versions exist of this *gagok* anthology compiled by Kim Su-jang during the reign of King Yeongjo. According to Pak's version, this anthology was initiated in 1754 and finished the following year, but it was revised and supplemented later.

The anthology is arranged by author, divided between known and unknown authors. Like *Cheongguyeongeon*, music is also included, but the number of pieces and poems differ between versions.

· *Gagokwollyu* 가곡원류 (歌曲源流)

Park Hyo-gwan and An Min-yeong compiled this one book, one volume *gagok* anthology during the fourteenth year of the reign of King Gojong (1876). There exist ten different versions; the version held by the National Gukak Center is considered to be the original. According to one of the other versions, the book is also known as *Cheongguyeongeon, Cheongguakjang, Haedongakjang*, and

Hwawonakbo.

The title *Gagokwollyu* has been mistakenly used since the word appeared in the preface, which made a citation from the *Gagokwollyu* part of the book *Neunggaejaemallok* by O–jeung of the Song Dynasty. The National Gukak Center version is divided into subsections *Nongokjieum, Gakjochaegyeok, Gajipung-dohyeongyongsipojomok, Maehwajeomjangdan,* and *Janggojangdanjeomsubaepo* along with *Gagokwollyu,* and contains a total of 856 *gagok* texts, including 665 male and 191 female pieces. Most of the songs include *yeoneumpyo* 연음표(連音標) graphic notation with melodic flows and special expressions beside the text.

· *Yeochanggayorok* 여창가요록(女唱歌謠錄)

Both year and author are unknown for this one book song anthology manuscript written in Korean. The volume contains a total of 182 texts with Korean titles like *Makdeuneun Jajeunhanip* and *Jungheorideuneun Jajeunhanip.* While a few variants exist, the Toyo (東洋) Collection version contains *yeoneumpyo* symbols next to the texts. This book is an anthology of female *gagok* works from *Gagokwollyu.* Thus, the number and order of the pieces are almost identical with the female vocal section in *Gagokwollyu.*

· *Hyeopryuldaeseong* 협율대성(協律大成)

No year or author are recorded for this one volume manuscript. The contents are divided into *yanggeum* notation and *yeongeonjeonbu* (*gagok* texts). The notation section contains playing techniques for the *yanggeum,* figures and parts of the *yanggeum,* and *Yeomillak, Bonhwanip, Sehwanip,* and *Pyeongjohoesang,* plus scores for *yanggeum* accompaniment to *ujo* and *gyemyeonjo gagok*.

The *gagok* part contains descriptions of *yeoneumpyo* notation, song expressions, *gagok* rhythmic patterns, and the text of 828 male and female *gagok* with *yeoneumpyo* notation. The end of the book includes the text of twelve *gasa* pieces, including *Eobusa*, *Cheosaga*, *Sangsabyeolgok*, *Chunmyeongok*, *Baekgusa*, and *Gwonjuga*, as well as text for currently–extinct *gasa* repertoire, including *Myeonggiga* and *Gwandongbyeolgok*. Text of *Taepyeongga* for female voice is also contained at the end of the book. This anthology, one of the variants of *Gagok-wollyu*, is very important to the study of *gagok* since it includes music notation as well as *gagok* text.

· *Geumhapjabo* 금합자보 (琴合字譜)

This single block volume contains *geomun-go* notation compiled by An Sang in 1572, the fifth year of King Seonjo. The title of the book is *Geumbo*, often referred to as *Ansanggeumbo*. The oldest existing *geomun-go* notation, it was designated as National Treasure number 283.

The music of the *geomun-go* is notated using *hapjabo*, *oeumyakbo*, and *yukbo* notation, while the music for *jeok* (flute) is in *oeumyakbo*; *janggu* and *buk* (percussion) are notated with drawings, and song texts are also notated. *Gagok*-related pieces in the book include *Pyeongjomandaeyeop*, *Pyeongjobukjeon*, *Ujobukjeon*, and *Bipamandaeyeop*.

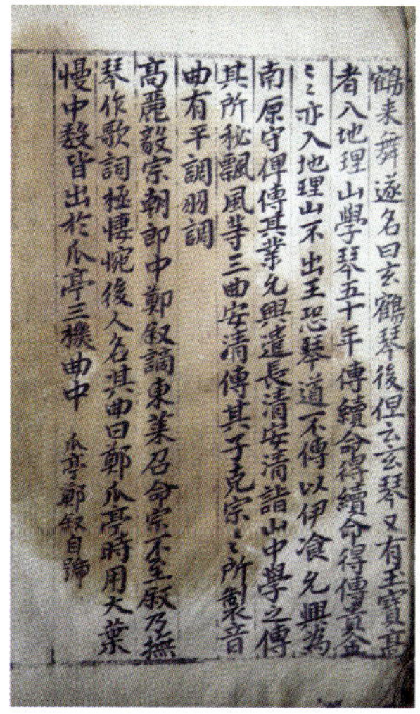

Yanggeumsinbo

· ***Yanggeumsinbo*** 양금신보 (梁琴新譜)

Yang Deok-su compiled this single block book of *geomun-go* notation in 1610, the second year of Gwanghaegun. The *geomun-go* music is notated using *hapjabo* and *yukbo* notation, with the song texts or the five tones of *gung*, *sang*, *gak*, *chi*, and *wu* to the right of *hapjabo*.

The book contains early *daeyeop*-related pieces as well as *jungdaeyeop* in four different modes. In the footnotes, it remarks that *sakdaeyeop* is not notated in the book since it is used for dance accompaniment.

· ***Sinjeunggeumbo*** 신증금보 (新證琴譜)

Also known as *Hyeongeumsinjeunggaryeong* or *Geumbosinjeunggaryeong*, this volume contains *geomun-go* notation compiled by Sin Seong in 1680, the sixth year of Sukjong. Besides *Yeomillak, Boheoja,* and *Yeongsanhoesang,* it also holds a diverse repertoire of *Jungdaeyeop* and *Sakdaeyeop* notation. *Gagok*-related pieces include *Pyeongjo Mandaeyeop (Jangdaeyeop), Pyeongjo Jungdaeyeop 1·2·3, Pyeongjo Bukjeon, Pyeongjo Sakdaeyeop 1·2·3, Pyeongjogyemyeonjo Jungdaeyeop 1·2·3, Pyeongjogyemyeonjo Bukjeon, Pyeongjogyemyeonjo Sakdaeyeop 1·2·3, Ujo Jungdaeyeop 1·3, Ujo Bukjeon, Ujo Gyemyeonjosakdaeyeop 2·3, Ujo Gyemyeonjo Jungdaeyeop 1·2, Ujo Sakdaeyeop 2·3, Pyeongjo Joeum,* and *Ujo Joeum.* A few pages are missing, but this is very important notation illustrating the diversification process of *Jungdaeyeop* and *Sakdaeyeop.*

· **Hangeumsinbo** 한금신보 (韓琴新譜)

Geomun-go notation compiled by Han Lip in 1724, its music is presented using *hapjabo* and *yukbo* notation. The book contains all *Mandaeyeop, Jungdaeyeop,* and *Sakdaeyeop* repertoire, and shows diverse *Jungdaeyeop* and *Sakdaeyeop* repertoires in different modes. *Gagok*-related repertoires in this book include *Mandaeyeop, Pyeongjo Jungdaeyeop 1·2·3, Pyeongjo Bukjeon 1·2, Pyeongjo Sakdaeyeop 1·2·3, Ujo Jungdaeyeop 1·2·3, Ujo Bukjeon 1·2, Ujo Sakdaeyeop 1·2·3·4, Pyeongjo Gyemyeonjo Jungdaeyeop 1·2·3, Pyeongjo Gyemyeonjo Bukjeon 1·2, Pyeongjo Gyemyeonjo Sakdaeyeop 1·2·3, Ujo Gyemyeonjo Bukjeon 1·2,* and *Ujo Gyemyeonjo Sakdaeyeop 1·2·3·4.*

· **Nangongsinbo** 낭옹신보 (浪翁新譜)

Kim Seong-gi and his disciples compiled this single volume of *geomun-go* notation in 1728. The *pungnyu-bang* repertoire includes *Yeongsanhoesang; Jung-*

daeyeop and *Sakdaeyeop* in *pyeongjo* and *pyeongjo gyemyeonjo* modes are also present.

The notation covers *Mandaeyeop* in *pyeongjo* mode, *Simbanggok*, three pieces of *Jungdaeyeop*, *Hujeonghwa*, three *Sakdaeyeop* pieces, three *Jungdaeyeop* pieces in *pyeongjo gyemyeonjo* mode, *Hujeonghwa*, three pieces of *Sakdaeyeop*, and *Joeum*. It is presumed that a few pages of *ujo* and *ujo gyemyeonjo* mode pieces, assumed to be originally part of the book, are missing.

· ***Eoeunbo*** 어은보 (漁隱譜)

This one-volume manuscript consists of *geomun-go* notation transcribed by Yu Gyeong-si in 1719. The book is notated using *hapjabo* and *yukbo*, and most of the parts seem to be copied from the book *Nangongsinbo*.

Gagok-related pieces include *Joeum*, *Jungdaeyeop* and *Sakdaeyeop* in four different modes, and *Bukjeon*.

· ***Yuyeji*** 유예지 (遊藝志)

This book of notation, compiled by Seo Yu-gu during King Sunjo's reign, is part of *Imwongyeongjeji*, vols. 91–98. The book contains *hyeongeumjabo* (*geomun-go* score), *danggeumjabo* (an ancient zither score), *yanggeumjabo* (dulcimer score), and *saenghwangjabo* (mouth organ score). *Gagok*-related pieces include *Ujungdaeyeop*, *Uchoyeop*, *Uiyeop*, *Usamyeop*, *Gyejungdaeyeop*, *Gyechoyeop*, *Gyeiyeop*, *Gyesamyeop*, *Nongyeop*, *Urak*, *Gyerak*, *Pyeonsudaeyeop*, *Pyeongujo*, *Pyeonggyejo*, *Samjungdaeyeop*, and *Hujeonghwa* in the *Hyeongeumjabo* section. Several pieces are also contained in the *Yanggeumjabo* and *Saenghwanjabo* parts. This book contains all *so-gagok*, *nong*, *nak*, and *pyeon*.

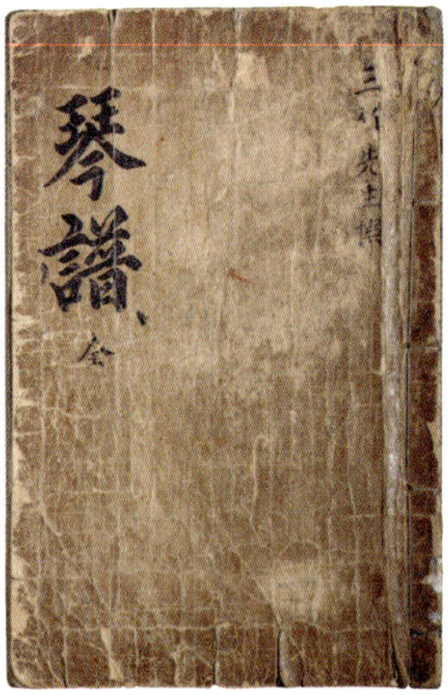

Samjukgeumbo

· ***Samjukgeumbo*** 삼죽금보 (三竹琴譜)

This is *geomun-go* notation, presumably compiled by Yi Seung-mu in 1841. It is notated in *jeongganbo* and *yukbo*. The *gagok*-related pieces comprise *sakdaeyeop*-related works, including *Ujo Chosudaeyeop, Ujo Jorim, Ujo Samsudaeyeop, Ujo Isudaeyeop, Ujo Soyongi, Urong, Gyemyeon Chosudaeyeop, Gyemyeon Isudaeyeop, Gyemyeon Jorim, Gyemyeon Samsudaeyeop, Gyemyeon Soyong, Gyemyeonjo Nong, Gyemyeonjo Eollong, Gyemyeon Naksijo, Ujo Naksijo, Ujo Eollak, Ujo Pyeollak, Gyemyeonjo Pyeonsudaeyeop, Gyemyeonjo Cheongseong Sakdaeyeop*, and *Pyeonggyemyeonjo Sakdaeyeop*, as well as *Jundaeyeop*-related pieces including *Ujo Chojungdaeyeop, Ujo Ijungdaeyeop, Ujo Samjungdaeyeop, Gyemyeonchojungdaeyeop, Gyemyeonijingdaeyeop, Gyemyeon Samjungdaeyeop, Ujohujeonghwa* (*Bukjeon*), and *Gyemyeon Hujeonghwa*. Other repertoire of *gasa* and *sijo* is also notated.

· ***Hyeongeumoeumtongron*** 현금오음통론 (玄琴五音統論)

This set of *geomun-go* notation compiled by Yun Yong-gu in 1886 contains *Yeongsanhoesang* and *gagok*. The *gagok*-related pieces include *Ujo Chosudaeyeop, Isudaeyeop, Junggeo, Pyeonggeo, Dugeo, Samsudaeyeop, Gyemyeon Chosudaeyeop, Soyongi, Yuldang, Eollong, Pyeongrong, Gyerak, Urak, Eollak, Pyeollak,*

Pyeon, and *Hwangyerak*. This volume provides evidence that *gagok* from this period is the basis of the currently–transmitted *gagok*.

Kim Yeong-gi, Important Intangible Cultural Heritage Holder – Female *Gagok*

Music and Performance Practice of *Gagok*

Music and Performance Practice of *Gagok*

1. Structure of *Gagok*

Structure of *gagok* can be divided into two parts, vocal part to sing *sijo* poetry and instrumental accompaniment parts of *daeyeoeum* (prelude or postlude) and *jungyeoeum* (interlude). The song part is divided into five sections that distinguished from *sijo* singing which consists of three sections even though two genres share three lines *sijo* poetry as text.

Structure of *Gagok*	Texts	Structure of *Sijo*
First section	Dongchangi Balganneunya	Initial Section
Second section	Nogojiri Ujijinda	
Third section	Sochineun ahinomeun sanggi ani ileotneunya	Middle Section

Structure of *Gagok*	Texts	Structure of *Sijo*
Fourth section	Jae neomeo	Final Section
Fifth section	Saraeginbateul eonjaegalryeo heoneuni	

Instrumental parts take roles of prelude, interlude or postlude. Originally instrumental parts was postlude of one individual piece, however when song–cycle tradition is firmly established, instrumental parts functioned as interlude and prelude. At current performance practice, when one or two pieces of song–cycle are performed, instrumental part functions as prelude. Thus it is placed in the first section in most of songs. However, two first songs *Ujo chosudaeyeop* and *Gyemyeon Chosudaeyeop* have a separate *daseureum* prelude part. *Taepyeongga*, the final piece of song–cycle does not begin with *daeyeoeum.*

<Figure 2> shows the basic structure of *gagok* with numbers of beats and rhythmic cycle with example of *Ujo Chosudaeyeop* (*Dongchangi…*) for male voice.

<Figure 2> Text Setting in Male *Gagok Ujo Chosudaeyeop* (*Dongchang-i*)

First	dong chang			i								Balgat				
				neu								nya				
Second	nogo			ji					ri			u	ji			
	jin			da												
Third												so	chi	neun		

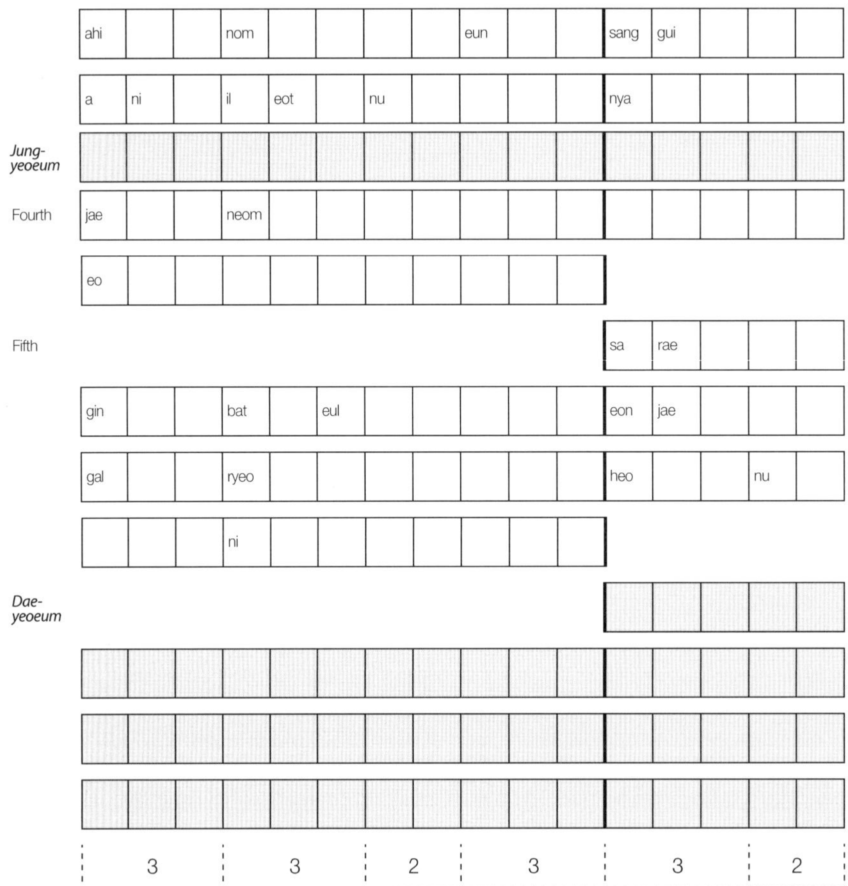

As shown in above, the basic structure of one *gagok* piece is total 16 *jangdans*. One *jangdan* (rhythmic cycle) comprises of 16 beats which referred as one unit. One unit *daegang* can be divided into 16 *jeonggan* (squares) and 6 *daegang* (bold line groupings), and 16 beats again is divide into 3.2.3.3.2.3 sub–beat units with bold lines of *daegang*. This rhythmic structure is also important in form of text phrasing. Mostly syllable phrasing beats are 1, 4, 9, 12, 15, the

Kim Yeong-gi, Important Intangible Cultural Heritage Holder – Female *Gagok*

first beat of each *daegang*. However, the irregular *gagok* which proceeds or shortens 45 syllables of regular *sijo*, allow more freedom. When the first word is comprised with two syllables (which referred as "two syllables head"), the first three beats are often omitted. When the too much syllables are provided, eight–beat melodies should be added in the third or fifth sections. Other special case can be found in the piece *Soyong*, singer is continuously sing vocalized syllable even during *jeongyeoeum* interlude part without stopping song.

2. Rhythmic Cycles of *Gagok*

Gagok employs two types of rhythmic cycle (*jangdan*), a 16-beat regular rhythm and a 10-beat condensed rhythm. The former is used in slower songs and the latter, which is also called the *pyeon jangdan*, in faster songs. Even though the total numbers of beats are 16, but *janggu* hits (*janggu jeom*) only 10 beats, and it is called as 10 *jeom*. *Jangdan* of *gagok* is played on the hourglass drum, *janggu* and basically should play on the soft sound part, *byeonjuk*, the rim of the drum with stick. However few pieces like *Pyeollak* and *Taepyeongga* plays the middle part of the drum to make a louder sound.

Basic *Jangdan* Structure of *Gagok* (16-beat regular rhythm)

⦶		⋮	○		|	i		○		•	⦶		⋮	○	•

16-beat unit of *gagok jangdan* shows its strong relationship with the music of early Joseon period as notated in music notation books of *Sejosillok Akbo* and *Siyonghyangakbo*. This means current *gagok* has evolved from *daeyeop*–related pieces of the early Joseon period.

One of the characteristics of *gagok jangdan* is division of one *jangdan* into two parts. One 16-beat unit can be divided into two beginnings, beat 1 and beat 12, where *hapjangdan* (play both sides of the drum) plays. It is called as *oengak* (complete section) from beat 1 to beat 11 or *seon* 7 *jeom* (former 7 beats), and the rest from beat 12-16 is called as *bangak* (half section) or hu 3 *jeom* (latter 3 beats). This rhythmic structure of *gagok jangdan* shows *gagok* begins the third *daegang* among 6 *daegangs* (3, 2, 3, 3, 2, 3).

A 10 *jeom* 16-beat regular *jangdan* is performed slowly. The first song *Chosudaeyeop* consists of 40 beats per minute, and the slowest song *Isudaeyeop* 20 beats per minute. After *Isudaeyeop*, following songs are getting faster. *Junggeo, Pyeonggeo*, and *Dugeo* are getting faster and *Dugeo* has similar tempo as *Chosudaeyeop*. *Samsudaeyeop* takes 45 beats per minutes. Following pieces like *Soyong* and other *nong* and *nak* pieces, tempo reaches 60 beats per minute. When the song–cycle reaches *pyeon* style which sings *saseol sijo*, tempo also becomes faster, 70 beats per minute. At the same time, not only tempo changes, but also *jangdan* of *gagok* changes in *pyeon* style repertoires.

16-beat rhythm

⦶		⋮	○				i		○		·	⦶		⋮	○	·

16-beat rhythm

⦶	⋮	○			i	○	·	⦶	⋮	○

A 10 *jeom* 10–beat *jangdan* is condensed rhythm and is also called the *pyeon jangdan* or *yeokneun jangdan*. The pieces with *pyeon jangdan* are faster in tempo, changes in *jangdan* and text phrasing and the atmosphere of the piece is cheerful. In the following shows text phrasing of *pyeon jangdan* piece *Pyeonsudaeyeop*. The melodic structure of the most of *gagok* pieces are melismatic style while *Pyeonsudaeyeop* shows syllabic or neumatic style text phrasing.

Text Setting in *Pyeonsudaeyeop* (*Cheongeumjunma*)

First	cheon	geum	jun	ma	ro			hwan	so	cheop
			heo	yeo						
Second	so	jwa	jo	an				garak		mae
	ro		da							
Third								geo	bang	e
	cheuk	gwa	ilho		ju	ho	go	bong		saeng
	yong	gwan	haeng	sang	choe	ro		da		
Jung-yeoeum										
Fourth	seoju		jak					yeok	sa	
	dang		a							
Fifth								i	baek	i
			yeo	i				dong	sa	
	saeng		eul					heo		yeo
			ra							
Dae-yeoeum										
	2		2		1	2		2		1

The tempi of current *gagok* repertoire appeared in *Namchanggagokbaek-seon* compiled by Kim Ki-su are as follows.

1 minutes 20 beats *Isudaeyeop*

1 minutes 24 beats *Junggeo*

1 minutes 30 beats *Pyeonggeo, Taepyeongga*

1 minutes 40 beats *Chosudaeyeop, Dugeo*

1 minutes 45 beats *Samsudaeyeop*

1 minutes 50 beats *Soyongi, Eollong, Pyeongrong, Urong*

1 minutes 55 beats *Urak, Gyerak*

1 minutes 60 beats *Eollak*

1 minutes 70 beats *Pyeollak, Pyeonsudaeyeop, Eonpyeon, Upyeon*

1 minutes 80 beats *Banyeop*

Like in regular *jangdan*, *pyeon jangdan*'s former 7–beat is called *oengak* and the latter 3–beat is called *bangak*. Both regular and *pyeon jangdan* comprise one *jangdan* with two 8–beats or 5–beats with five *janggu jeom*. Thus the smallest unit for *gagok jangdan* is 8–beat (5–beat in *pyeon jangdan*) and when the melody is extended with increased texts, music prolonged based on an 8–beat unit. The *jangdan* and tempi of *gagok* was explained with *maehwajeom jangdan* and *yangsikcheok* theory in old notation books. *Maehwajeom jangdan* employs three *yin–jeoms* and two *yang–jeoms* to describe half *jangdan of gagok* (8–beat). The old scores wrote that repetition of *maehwajeom jangdan* (5–*jeoms*) might correspond to *gagok jangdan*. *Gagokwollyu*, especially, employ *yin* and *yang*

Park Mun-gyu with *Janggu*

jeoms to describe the *gagok jangdan*.

Yangsikcheok was the standard of measurement based on the pulse and a breath of a healthy adult man to measure the time of one entire piece of *gagok* performance. Thus in case of *Isudaeyeop*, three pulses correspond to one beat, six pulses to two beats, one *sik*. Thus it takes 48 pulses (8 *sik*) to complete one *jangdan*.

3. *Gagok* Modes

The modes in current *gagok* are of two types, *ujo* and *gyemyeonjo*. *Ujo* originally referred to *ujo pyeongjo*, and *gyemyeonjo* to *ujo gyemyeonjo*. In these cases, *ujo* means "upper" and *pyeongjo* and *gyemyeonjo* are mode types. Upper and lower modes were played together during the Joseon Dynasty when *Mandaeyeop*, *Jungdaeyeop*, and *Sakdaeyeop* were performed. However, the low modes gradually disappeared in the late Joseon period while the upper mode remained. Thus, current *gagok* are only in the *ujo* (upper) mode. The central tone of the *ujo* mode is *hwangjong* (eb). *Pyeongjo* in mode comprises the five tones, *hwangjong–taeju–jungryeo–imjong–namryeo*, while *gyemyeonjo* comprises *hwangjong–hyeopjong–jungryeo–imjong–muyeok*. However, *hyeopjong* and *namryeo* are relatively less important, and thus three tones became the major tones for the melody. The current repertoire of *ujo gagok* includes pieces in order from *Ujo Chosudaeyeop* to *Ujo Soyong* and the *so–gagok Urong, Urak, Eollak*, and *Upyeon*. The repertoire of *gyemyeonjo* includes pieces in order from *Gyemyeon Choseudaeyeop* to *Gyemyeon Soyong* and the *so–gagok* pieces *Eollong, Pyeongrong, Gyerak, Pyeonsudaeyeop, Eollpyeon*, and *Taepyeongga*. Some pieces, like *Banyeop, Pyeollak*, and *Hwangyerak*, employ two different modes (*banu bangye*), the first half in *ujo* and the second half in *gyemyeonjo*. These pieces begin in *ujo* mode but soon change to *gyemyeonjo* in the third line or *jungyeoeum* interlude section. *Gyerak* and *Pyeongrong* are not called *banu bangye*, but these pieces begin in *gyemyeonjo* and change to *ujo* in the fifth line, and are followed by a piece in *ujo* mode.

The register of *gagok* usually does not exceed two octaves. The highest note of the melody is *cheongjungryeo*. The lowest notes for *ujo* and *gyemyeonjo* differ; in *ujo*, it is *taktaeju*, and in *gyemyeonjo*, it is *takjungryeo*. The highest and lowest notes are rarely employed.

4. *Gagok* Vocal Style

The principal techniques of vocal production in the classical traditions of *gagok*, *gasa*, and *sijo*, involve the chest voice using abdominal breathing. Professional *gagok* singers call this technique "*dwitmokeul sseunda*" (using the back throat). This technique produces a strong sound and a consistent tone color. Unlike male singers who employ the chest voice, the female voice is characterized by a high–pitched *soksori* (inner voice), *sesong* (fine voice), and *gaseong* (falsetto), the latter falsetto vocal technique also employed by *gasa* and *sijo*.

One of the characteristics of *gagok* vocal techniques is the pronunciation of vowels. For example, the vowel "a" (아) can be pronounced "a–eu" (아으). Similarly, diphthongs can be transformed into a series of related vowels, for example, "ae" (애) and "ui" (의) can be pronounced "a.ui.i" (아으이) and "ui.i" (으이). In the case of sustaining vowels on different notes in melismatic style, the aspiration "h" is added to pronounce "ha" (하) or "hu" (후). This phonetic treatment adds special timbral effects to classical vocal music. Idiomatic expressions are different in *ujo* and *gyemyeonjo* modes. *Ujo* produces a heavy and serene sound with wide vibrato, while *gyemyeonjo* produces a soft and narrow vibrato.

Important Intangible Cultural Heritage Holder Kim Gyeong-bae, singing *Gagok*

Important Intangible Cultural Heritage Holder Kim Yeong-gi, singing *Gagok*

5. Performance Style of *Gagok*

Gagok is performed by a solo male or female voice, accompanied by an instrumental chamber ensemble. Only *Taepyeongga*, the last piece of the song cycle, is performed as a male–female duet. A standard ensemble would include *geomun–go*, *gayageum* (12–stringed zither), *daegeum* (a transverse bamboo flute), *sepiri* (bamboo oboe), *haegeum* (2–stringed spiked fiddle), and *janggu*; often, *danso* (a short bamboo flute) and *yanggeum* are added while *saenghwang* was used in the old days. The melodies of instrumental accompaniment mostly follow the melodic line of the song, but the playing techniques and timbre of each instrument add special effects. The melodies of *geomun–go*

Important Intangible Cultural Heritage Holder Jo Sun-ja and Teaching Assistant Lee Dong-gyu, singing Male–Female *Gagok*

and *yanggeum* are mostly documented in the old notation books. A few *gaya-geum* scores exist, but no wind score has been found. Thus, music scores for wind instruments are twentieth–century transcriptions of oral tradition.

Nowadays, *gagok* is performed in a concert hall, and male and female singers sing alternately. Often, male and female singers individually sing only male or female repertoire, respectively. Usually, *gagok* is performed as a complete song cycle, from the first piece, *Chosudaeyeop*, to the last piece, *Taepyeongga*, in succession, without any pause between songs, as the male and female singers alternate. In general, the male voice was sung solo while the female voice was sung by more than two singers. A strict rule governs performance of the complete *gagok* cycle.

<Table 3> shows the order of pieces in the *gagok* cycle, for the different cases of male and female alternate singing, male voice alone, and female voice alone.

<Table 3> Order of the *Gagok* Cycle

Male and Female voice	Male Voice only	Female Voice only
Male *Ujo Chosudaeyeop*	*Ujo Chosudaeyeop*	*Ujo Isudaeyeop*
Female *Ujo Isudaeyeop*	*Ujo Isudaeyeop*	*Ujo Junggeo*
Male *Ujo Junggeo*	*Ujo Junggeo*	*Ujo Pyeonggeo*
Female *Ujo Junggeo*	*Ujo Pyeonggeo*	*Ujo Dugeo*
Male *Ujo Pyeonggeo*	*Ujo Dugeo*	*Banyeop*
Female *Ujo Pyeonggeo*	*Ujo Samsudaeyeop*	*Gyemyeonjo Isudaeyeop*
Male *Ujo Samsudaeyeop*	*Ujo Soyong*	*Gyemyeonjo Junggeo*
Female *Ujo Dugeo*	*Banyeop*	*Gyemyeonjo Pyeonggeo*
Male *Ujo Soyong*	*Gyemyeonjo Chosudaeyeop*	*Gyemyeonjo Dugeo*
Female *Banyeop*	*Gyemyeonjo Isudaeyeop*	*Pyeollong*
Male *Gyemyeonjo Chosudaeyeop*	*Gyemyeonjo Junggeo*	*Urak*
Female *Gyemyeonjo Isudaeyeop*	*Gyemyeonjo Pyeonggeo*	*Hwangyerak*
Male *Gyemyeonjo Junggeo*	*Gyemyeonjo Dugeo*	*Gyerak*
Female *Gyemyeonjo Junggeo*	*Gyemyeonjo Samsudaeyeop*	*Pyeonsudaeyeop*
Male *Gyemyeonjo Pyeonggeo*	*Gyemyeonjo Soyong*	*Taepyeongga*
Female *Gyemyeonjo Pyeonggeo*	*Eollong*	
Male *Gyemyeonjo Samsudaeyeop*	*Pyeollong*	
Female *Gyemyeonjo Dugeo*	*Gyerak*	
Male *Eollong*	*Urak*	
Female *Pyeollong*	*Eollak*	
Male *Gyerak*	*Pyeollak*	
Female *Gyerak*	*Pyeonsudaeyeop*	
Male *Eollak*	*Eolpyeon*	
Female *Urak*	*Urong*	
Male *Pyeollak*	*Upyeon*	
Female *Pyeonsudaeyeop*	*Taepyeongga*	
Duet *Taepyeongga*		
Total 27 songs	**26 songs**	**15 songs**

A full, two–singer performance would begin with a free rhythm instrumental tuning piece, *daseureum*, and move to the first piece, *Chosudaeyeop*. The last piece, *Taepyeongga*, with no prelude, would begin with a *geomun–go* solo of about eleven beats of the first line.

A short *gagok* performance with one or two songs would begin with *daeyeoeum* as prelude. *Daeyeoeum*, originally a postlude, often functions as a prelude for complete or shortened performances. In this case, the final fifth beat of the *daeyeoeum* instrumental is omitted and the song begins, then only the *janggu* begins from the sixth beat, while the *geomun–go* and *gayageum* begin from the ninth beat, followed by other instruments at the twelfth beat.

6 . Expressions of *Gagok*

In the book *Gagokwollyu*, a section called "gajipungdo hyeongyong" is devoted to explaining the musical features and expression of each *gagok* song. The descriptions are made up of four Chinese characters grouped into two phrases, providing the singer with some stanzas as guidance on how to express the nature of the song. These are summarized as follows.

Chosudaeyeop	Dancing with long sleeves, with green willow leaves flying in spring wind
Isudaeyeop	Confucius preaches under a ginkgo tree, rain and wind are soft and constant
Samsudaeyeop	The general goes to a battle, a dancing sword kills the villain
Soyong	Strong wind blows in a tempest, it is swaying like a swallow
Pyeon Soyong	Two generals confront each other, they are masters of the spear
Manheong (Eollong)	Scholars debate, in multiple voices like the wind and clouds
Nongga	A clear stream carries a strip of silk, bobbing up and down
Naksijo	The world is peaceful, like a spring day when flowers bloom

Pyeon Naksijo	This world is chaos, as when Cho and Han battled each other
Pyeonsudaeyeop	Sounds like army troops marching this way, with drums and trumpets roaring

Musical Characteristics of Individual Pieces and Lyrics

Musical Characteristics of Individual Pieces and Lyrics

1. *Namchang Gagok* (Male Voice)

Present–day *gagok* are divided into songs for female voice and male voice. However, this distinction does not appear in the record until the beginning of the nineteenth century. As the century progressed, more and more *gagok* were written for female singers than for male, and the distinction by gender became clearly marked. This leads us to assume that *gagok* up through the eighteenth century was primarily for male singers. In current *gagok*, repertoires for male voice contain twenty–six songs. The following are detailed descriptions of each piece.

1) *Ujo Chosudaeyeop*

This song is called *choetchi* since it is the first song of the entire *gagok* song cycle. *Gagok* is sung by male and female singers, in alternation, and *Chosudaeyeop* is for men, not women. *Chosudaeyeop* in the *ujo* mode is built on the *hwangjong* (黃, Eb) *-taeju* (太, F) *-jungryeo* (仲, Ab) *-yimjong* (林, Bb) *-namryeo* (南, C) pentatonic scale, with the *jungryeo* note stretched. The tempo is 40 beats per minute. The song lays the foundation for the rest of the songs in terms of rhythmic structure, form, and syllabication. Thus, it can be understood as the "original song." As lyrics, it employs a typical *sijo* poem. According to *Gagokwollyu*, the feeling of this song is described as "dancing with long sleeves,

Important Intangible Cultural Heritage Holder Kim Gyeong-bae, singing *Ujo Chosudaeyeop*

with green willow leaves flying in spring wind." Below is the text of *Ujo Chosudaeyeop*.

> East window is dawning nightingale singing
> Ye cowboys are you yet sleeping?
> Your field awaits plowing.

2) *Ujo Isudaeyeop*

This song is called *Duljjechi* since it is the second song of the entire *gagok* song cycle. It is the slowest of the songs, at 20 beats per minute, and it is called *gingeot,* the long one. The melodic structure of *Isudaeyeop* is similar to that in the two subsequent songs, *Junggeo* and *Pyeonggeo.* Compared to *Chosudaeyeop,* this song begins in a very low pitch register. *Gagokwollyu* says of the expression of the piece, "Confucius preaches under a ginkgo tree, rain and wind are soft and constant." The text follows.

> I said I shall return to nature, yet I am working these ten years.
> Wild geese that know nothing of this still await my return.
> After I have served my lord, I shall return to you.

3) *Ujo Junggeo*

This song is called *Jungheori* or *jungheorideuneun jajeun hanip.* It exists in both male and female versions, and can be viewed as a relatively recent variation on *Isudaeyeop*. *Junggeo* is sung at the tempo of 25 beats per minute, which is slightly faster than *Isudaeyeop*. The melody rises in the mid–section of the first stanza and also in the third and fifth stanzas.

> I love my neighbors, that is my rock; I care for my parents and my king, that is my pillar.
>
> Both duty and virtue fill my heart.
>
> Our country will never falter in the wind.

4) *Ujo Pyeonggeo*

Pyeonggeo is also called *Makdeuneun jajeunhanip*. This song was created, based on *Isudaeyeop*, in the latter part of the nineteenth century and therefore has many melodies that have been derived from it. As the title *Pyeonggeo* indicates, the melody begins in the high register, like *Chosudaeyeop*. The tempo is 30 beats per minute.

> Lucky star and clouds in the sky, the world is bright and nice.
>
> Rites, music, and culture of ancient times bloom again.
>
> Make wine with the ocean and let us get drunk, my brothers.

Important Intangible Cultural Heritage Holder Kim Gyeong-bae, singing *Ujo Dugeo*

5) *Ujo Dugeo*

Other names for *Dugeo* are *Joim* or *Deuleonaeneungeot* (high register in the beginning); it was also called *JonJajinhanip* or *SoSakdaeyeop* in old notation books. *Ujo Dugeo* shares melodic features with *Ujo Isudaeyeop*, with the *jungryeo* and *taeju* notes prolonged. One feature that is different from *Ujo Isudaeyeop* is that the beginning note is a higher pitch in *Namryeo*, which is the reason that it is called *Dugeo* (head–high). The tempo is 40 beats per minute.

Clouds have no thoughts, that is a lie.

They roam around everywhere.

Why, of all places, stand before the sun?

6) *Ujo Samsudaeyeop*

This song is called *Sejjechi* since it is the third song following *Chosudaeyeop* and *Isudaeyeop*; it is only sung in the male voice. Its melodic register is higher than the proceeding songs, ranging two octaves from *tak jungryeo* to *cheong jungryeo*. The tempo is 45 beats per minute. Its lyrics are a typical *sijo* poem. *Gagokwollyu* describes this song with "the general goes to a battle, a dancing sword kills the villain."

Spring flowers, do not lament your short lives.

You shall live again when spring comes again.

Alas our lives are but once.

7) *Ujo Soyong*

This song is also called *Soyongi* or *Samroe Soyongi*, meaning "to rattle, chatter, and rumble." It reduces melodies from *Samsudaeyeop*, and varies them an octave higher. *Soyong* is a song only for males; characteristically, the singing continues even during the interlude, *jungyeoeum*. The lyrics are an extended *sijo* poem, with tempo set at 50 beats per minute. In *Gagokwollyu*, this song is described with "strong wind blows in a tempest, swaying like a swallow." This song has been around since the mid–nineteenth century, judging from its inclusion in *Samjukgeumbo*. Its atmosphere is very cheerful.

> A pot that cooks by itself, a horse that runs without food,
> Fair wife who is also nimble, a kettle that pours out fresh water,
> A cow that lays good meat like an egg
> Give me these five and I shall be content.

8) *Banyeop*

This song is also called *Baneotsakdaeyeop*, with the first half in the *ujo* mode and the second half in *gyemyeon* mode. The word *Banyeop* indicates that it consists of two different modes, half–and–half. Therefore, words such as *bamyeot* or *baneolsakdaeyeop*, commonly used in old manuscripts or song anthologies, indicate the same characteristic. The reason that it uses two different modes has to do with the style of *gagok* singing at the time. A single collection of *gagok* consisted of twenty-six male and fifteen female songs, in *ujo* and *gyemyeonjo* mode, respectively. When performed, songs in *ujo* mode were sung first, until *Soyong* (*Dugeo* in the case of female singers), at which point the mode shifted to *gyemyeonjo*. Therefore, *Banyeop*, with its two different modes, acted as a bridge for such a mode change. In general, the last part of stanza three, or the third and fourth beats of *jungyeoeum*, would change to *gyemyeonjo*. The tempo is 80 beats per minute in the *ujo* section but the song becomes very slow in the *gyemyeonjo* part.

Flowers of all kinds, in spring, leaves of every color, in autumn

Wine is sweet, the moon hangs over the lake.

Wish to get drunk with pretty goblet, good wine, bright moon.

9) *Gyemyeonjo Chosudaeyeop*

This is called *Gyemyeonjo*, but its real mode is *ujo gyemyeonjo*. Three notes: *hwangjong* (黃, E♭) -*jungryeo* (仲, A♭) -*imjong* (林, B♭) are the most important in the melody, with the *imjong* note usually elongated.

Important Intangible Cultural Heritage Holder Kim Gyeong-bae, singing *Gyemyeon Chosudaeyeop*

I cross over cheongseokryeong, where is chohagu?

Cold northern wind, with strong rain

Who will notice me, in my present misery?

[a *sijo* by King Hyojong (17th in the Joseon Dynasty, 1649-1659) when taken hostage to China as the heir]

10) *Gyemyeonjo Isudaeyeop*

Gagokwollyu describes the program for this song as "Confucius preaches under a ginkgo tree, rain and wind are soft and constant."

Important Intangible Cultural Heritage Holder Kim Gyeong-bae, singing *Gyemyeon Samsudaeyeop*

In the twilight, birds come home and a new moon rises.

Monk who is crossing the log bridge

He hears bell ringing, is your temple still far?

11) *Gyemyeonjo Junggeo*

This song is also called *Jungheori* or *Jungheori deuneun Jajeunhanip* in *gyemyeonjo* mode. It comes in both male and female versions, and is a variation of *Isudaeyeop*, a relatively recent development. The tempo is 25 beats per minute, slightly faster than *Isudaeyeop*. The middle part of the first stanza is higher in pitch but is different from the one found in *Isudaeyeop* in that it has higher pitches also in the third and fifth stanzas.

Clean wind blows and I stand by the window wearing my simple hat

I rest leaning on my old pillow.

At sunset, boys felling trees come back whistling.

[a *sijo* referring to Yi Tae-baek's poem]

12) *Gyemyeonjo Pyeonggeo*

Pyeonggeo is also called *Makdeuneun Jajinhanip*. *Pyeonggeo* indicates that the first stanza begins, as in *Chosudaeyeop*, in a higher register.

I have lived 50 years, cannot go back

At least I wish to stay as I am right now.

Gray hair, would you please slow down?

13) *Gyemyenjo Dugeo*

This song is also called *Joim*, perhaps because the rapid speed of its melody makes it sound "tense." The title, *Dugeo*, means that the "head is lifted up." Its melodic features are the same as in *Isudaeyeop* in *gyemyeonjo* mode, but the notes *imjong* and *jungryeo* are elongated. Another difference is that it begins in the high *imjong*, which gives the song its name.

Important Intangible Cultural Heritage Holder Kim Gyeong-bae, singing *Gyemyeon Isudaeyeop*

I climb Akyangru and look down on Chilbaekri by Dongjeong lake.

Lonely bird rises above sunset, sky and water are tainted alike

Smell of fall fills the river and I hear a fisherman's trumpet.

[a *sijo* referring to a poem by Wangbal, a Chinese poet of the Dang Dynasty]

14) *Gyemyeonjo Samsakdaeyeop*

The melody of this song is higher than in preceding songs, with a tonal range of two octaves from *tak jungryeo* to *cheong jungryeo*. *Gagokwollyu* describes the program for this song as "the general goes to a battle, a dancing sword kills the villain."

At sunset I ride on my donkey drunk.

Long is the valley road, I have seen in my dream

Fisherman's trumpet awakes me from my dream.

15) *Gyemyeonjo Soyong*

The word, *soyongi*, means "to rattle, chatter, and rumble." This song shortened melodies from *Samsudaeyeop*, and then alters them by transposing them an octave higher. *Soyong* is a song only for males, in which characteristically the singing continues even during the interlude, *jungyeoeum*, in *iptaryeong*. The lyrics are an extended *sijo* poem, with tempo set at 50 beats per minute. *Gagokwollyu* evokes this song with "strong wind blows in a tempest, swaying like a swallow."

> My! who is this? Just a monk from that temple.
>
> Why have you come to such a lonely place?
>
> Just to hang my hat, over your hat.
>
> [a *sijo* from the late Joseon Dynasty; a satirical conversation between a man and a woman expressing mutual love]

16) *Eollong*

In the present title, *Eollong*, *eol* comes from *eon*, *eot*, or *eol*, and means "to use two different singing styles" and "to begin on a high, extended note." The beginning of this song is the same as in *Samsudaeyeop*, followed by deep vibrato. The initial extended high note should be sung heavily and austerely as in *Samsudaeyeop*, but from the second stanza forward, the style becomes more at ease, using vibration. Such use of two different singing styles is the reason this song is also called *banjagi* or *banjuk*. This song is a variation from *nong* and is sung only by a male singer. *Gagokwollyu* describes the program for this song as "scholars debate, in multiple voices like the wind and clouds." It has been around since the late nineteenth century, which is relatively recent for a *gagok* song. Its tempo is 50 beats per minute.

Important Intangible Cultural Heritage Holder Kim Gyeong-bae, singing *Eollong*

They say Yi Tae–baek was able to drink 300 glasses a day.

A macho man walks in the street and women throw tangerines.

No one can exceed these two in grace.

17) *Pyeongrong*

Pyeong in the title, *Pyeongrong*, means low. This is because, compared to *Eollong*, with its high beginning note, this song begins in the middle register. Its mode is *gyemyeonjo*, making use of *hwangjong*, *jungryeo*, and *imjong* as the most important notes. In versions with a longer text, the third and fifth stanzas could be extended. It is sung by both male and female singers, at a tempo of about 50 beats per minute.

A fall evening with full moon, riding a boat

I see the moon in water.

Why don't you pick it up and play with it?

18) *Gyerak*

This song belongs to the *nak* family of tunes, consisting of small *gagok*. The mode is *gyemyeonjo* and thus the song is called *Gyerak*. It is sung by both male and female singers. According to old sources, it was originally in pentatonic *gyemyeonjo*: *hwangjong–hyeopjong–jungryeo–imjong–muyeok*, but changed to having only three notes (*hwangjong–jungryeo–imjong*) after King Sunjo's time. The tempo is about 55 beats per minute. *Gagokwollyu* portrays its atmosphere as "the world is peaceful like a spring day when flowers bloom."

> With a thoroughbred, a hunting hawk, and a reliable bow
> You carefree man, hunting pheasants in the forest.
> We shall join you, after we have served our lord.

19) *Urak*

Urak means a *naksijo* in *ujo* mode. It is sung by both male and female singers. While *Eollak*, derived from *Urak* in male voice, begins on a high extended note, *Urak* begins on a low pitch. The mode is pentatonic *pyeongjo*, consisting of *hwangjong–taeju–jungryeo–imjong–namryeo*, and the main note is *hwangjong*. The tempo is about 55 beats per minute. *Gagokwollyu* describes it as "the world is peaceful like a spring day when flowers bloom."

> Lost my fishing pole while dozing, lost my coat while dancing.
> Do not laugh, wild goose, I am not getting too old
> I was just taken by spring flowers, that is all.

20) *Eollak*

While *Urak* begins on a low note, *Eollak*, also called "yelling *naksijo*," begins on a high extended note. It is sung only by a male singer and the mode

Important Intangible Cultural Heritage Holder Kim Gyeong-bae, singing *Urak*

is pentatonic *ujo* in *pyeongjo* style. The tempo is about 60 beats per minute, and the third and fifth stanzas can be extended if words are added.

> I thought I saw some shadow in moonlight, ran out, only to find myself alone.
> It was only the bird, pluming its feathers
> Thank god it was a dark night, lest I should have made a fool of myself.

21) *Pyeollak*

Pyeon in the title, *Pyeollak,* has two meanings. One is that the song has been reduced from 16 to 10 beats per rhythmic pattern, and the other is that the lyrics have been expanded, and thus the song is a *saseol sijo*. In other words, *pyeon* is "to bind" or "to narrate." This is also found in folk songs with more words, which are called *yeokkeum* or *saseol*. Therefore, *Pyeollak* is *naksijo* based on "bounded texts." The song is sung by a male singer only and features a transposition in the middle. The beginning part is in *ujo, pyeongjo* style, with *hwangjong–taeju–jungryeo–imjong–namryeo,* but the song changes to *gyemyeon* mode, with *hwangjong–jungryeo–imjong,* from the third stanza. Its rhythmic pattern is a *pyeon jangdan* of 10 beats, with the exception of a *daeyeo-eum* prelude, which is in 16 beats. The tempo begins with 70 beats per minute but slows down to 30 beats at the fourth stanza. The *janggo* accompaniment reflects this change, by beating on the center of the drum head.

Important Intangible Cultural Heritage Holder, Kim Gyeong-bae, singing *Pyeollak*

How wretched is the pheasant chased by a hawk in a bare mountain.
How desperate should the captain feel when seeing his boat floundering in an ocean storm.
But I am more wretched and desperate, having lost my beloved last night.

22) *Pyeonsudaeyeop*

This song exists in both female and male versions, and consists of *pyeon jangdan*, which has 10 beats for every rhythmic pattern. Its form is typical *gagok* form but the third and fifth stanzas can be extended, depending on the lyrics. The mode is *gyemyeonjo*. According to *Gagokwollyu*, this song "sounds like army troops marching this way, with drums and trumpets roaring."

Our country boasts of great landscapes
Seoul, situated within high mountains, is the home of happy people
Blessed is our lord, our king.

23) *Eolpyeon*

The title indicates that this song begins on a high and extended pitch, has lots of text, and consists of *pyeon jangdan* with 10 beats per rhythmic cycle. It originated in the late nineteenth century. The third and fifth stanzas can be extended when more text is added.

Cut down that pine tree, to make a small boat for our little outing, fill it with dancers, musicians, wine, and fruit.

Go out to Gyeongpodae

Let us all get drunk and enjoy the great sight.

24) *Urong*

When an entire collection of *gagok* is sung in one setting, a *Banyeop*, which consists of both *ujo* and *gyemyeonjo* sections, is used to bridge the transition from *ujo* to *gyemyeonjo*. A *Banyeop* begins in *ujo* mode but switches to *gyemyeonjo* at the *jungyeoeum* section. However, when there is no transposition and *ujo* is maintained by moving on to *Urak*, the mode is not changed and this is called *Urong*. This song is sung only by male singers and has a tempo of 50 *jeonggan* per minute. At present, there is only one *Urong* known.

Flowers of all kinds, in spring, leaves of every color, in autumn

Wine is sweet, a moon hangs over the lake.

Wish to get drunk with pretty goblet, good wine, bright moon.

25) *Upyeon*

Upyeon is *Jajinhanip* arranged in the *ujo* mode. There is only a male version and its rhythmic pattern is *pyeon jangdan* with 10 beats per cycle. The third and fifth stanzas can be extended when text is added.

I just saw a phoenix dancing in our pavilion, now it is gone.

Garden in the O Dynasty's palace is covered with weeds and great men of Jin are now in their graves.

Mountains far away are hidden behind Cheongcheon, and baekro wine divides water.

Everything is but a dream, hiding the sun.

We are worried not having found our city.

[a poem by Yi Tae-baek, a famous Chinese poet]

26) *Taepyeongga*

The reason this song is called *Taepyeongga* has to do with its lyrics. In *Jeongjaemudoholgi*, a book on court dance from the late Joseon Dynasty, lyrics with the name *Taepyeongga* are mentioned for the first time. *Taepyeongga* also appears in *Hwigeumgagokbo*, compiled by Yun Yong-gu, who was in charge of court banquets at the time. However, in a notation book called *Samjukgeumbo*, a late nineteenth century source, there is a piece entitled *Cheongseong Sakdaeyeop*, which is described in the footnotes as "another name for *gyemyeon Isudaeyeop* sung by both male and female singers." This leads us to assume that *Cheongseong Sakdaeyeop* or *Cheongseong Jajinhanip* is the original title for *Taepyeongga*. The form of this song is typical for *gagok*, except that the beginning of the first stanza is sung in *idu*, thus on the twelfth beat. Therefore, the text also omits *iryeodo* but begins on *taepyeongseongdae*. The *daeyeoeum* prelude is not there, but a *geomun–go* plays the first eleven beats of the first pattern as

Important Intangible Cultural Heritage Holder Kim Gyeong-bae and Trainee Candidate, singing *Taepyeongga*

a prelude, which is then followed by the other instruments and singing. The rhythmic pattern has 16 beats (ten *jeom*) per cycle, and the *janggo* player hits the edge of drum head until the fifth *jeom* of the fourth stanza, which is the seventh beat, when he moves to the center of the head. Then, from the seventh beat of the third pattern, in the fifth stanza, he returns to hitting the edge to come to a quiet ending. At present, there is only one text remaining for *Taepyeongga*, by Seong Su-chim, sung by Ha Gyu-il.

> We live in such a glorious period,
>
> Like the ancient peaceful days of China.
>
> Let us enjoy these good days.
>
> [often the final song in a banquet]

2 . *Yeochang Gagok* (Female Voice)

1) *Ujo Isudaeyeop*

Isudaeyeop is the first female voice song since female voice does not sing *Chosudaeyeop*. The slowest song in a *gagok* cycle, with 20 beats per minute, this piece begins on a low pitch. The musical atmosphere of this song is described as "Confucius preaches under a ginkgo tree, rain and wind are soft and constant." The rhythmic pattern has 16 beats (ten *jeom*) per cycle with basic structure.

Important Intangible Cultural Heritage Holder Jo Sun-ja, singing *Ujo Isudaeyeop*

Willow leaves turn into threads, the nightingale, into the loom

Until spring flowers turn summer-green I have shed my tears weaving.

My sorrow is still great, who said summer is merrier than spring?

2) *Ujo Junggeo*

This song is called *jungheori* or *jajinhanip*, "with a raised mid-section." As in the case of the male version, this song was also derived from *Isudaeyeop* in the late nineteenth century. Therefore, its melodic features share much in common with *Isudaeyeop*. *Junggeo*, in the female version especially, has lots of vibrato, inflection, and falsetto.

Bluebird, thank you for your good news.

How did you travel such a long road?

Did you read love in his heart?

3) *Ujo Pyeonggeo*

This song was also derived from *Isudaeyeop* in the late nineteenth century. This song is called "*jajinhanip* played lifted," since unlike *Isudaeyeop*, its original, which begins on a low pitch, it begins on a note in the middle register, like *Chosudaeyeop*. *Pyeonggeo* female in *ujo* mode characteristically begins with two syllables in the first stanza. Therefore, the first three beats of the first stanza are omitted and the song begins on the fourth beat.

Yangguibi's smile has enchanted the whole world.

King Hyeonjong was once her slave

I grieve the flowers at her pretty grave.

4) *Ujo Dugeo*

This was called *Joim*, *Jon Jajinhanip*, or *SoSakdaeyeop* in old notation book and anthologies. Its title, *Dugeo*, means "to lift the head," which refers to the raised pitch at the beginning of the first stanza. The rhythmic pattern has 16 beats (ten *jeom*) per cycle and its tempo is 40 beats per minute.

Important Intangible Cultural Heritage Holder Kim Yeong-gi, singing *Ujo Dugeo*

> If fifteen minutes is like three years, how long would seem ten whole days?
> When you are happy, you seldom think of other people grieving
> I lose my sleep, thinking of my love far away.

5) *Banyeop*

As its name suggests, the first half of this song is in *ujo* mode, while the second half is in *gyemyeonjo*. In other words, this song is in *banubangye*, in both *ujo* and *gyemyeonjo* mode. When the entire *gagok* cycle is sung, the female singer would move from *Dugeo*, in *ujo*, to a song in *gyemyeonjo*; between them is the point at which a song in *banubangye* is sung, to make the transition smooth. Its tempo is 90 beats per minute.

Never deliver other people's letters.
You may be able to tell half of the story
But how could I bring myself to read such an estranged epistle.

6) *Gyemyeonjo Isudaeyeop*

Isudaeyeop in *gyemyeonjo* is the second song of *gyemyeonjo gagok*. Since *gagok* for females has no *Chosudaeyeop*, this is the first song of the section. The rhythmic pattern has 16 beats (ten *jeom*) per cycle with basic structure and its tempo is 20 beats per minute.

Cherry blossoms are falling, and yet he has not come.
Could I trust the magpie who cried in the morning?
Yet I shall wait for him, having fixed my make-up.

7) *Gyemyeonjo Junggeo*

A variation of *Isudaeyeop* that appeared in the late nineteenth century, this song is also called *Jungheori* or *Jungheori deuneun Jajinhanip*. The rhythmic pattern has 16 beats (ten *jeom*) per cycle with basic structure and its tempo is 25 beats per minute.

Important Intangible Cultural Heritage Holder Jo Sun-ja, singing *Gyemyeon Junggeo*

Sun is setting and the world is turning dark

Moon rises, night flower blooms, I think of him even more.

Owl, whom do you pine for all night?

8) *Gyemyeonjo Pyeonggeo*

Derived from *Isudaeyeop*, this song is also called *Makdeuneun Jajinhanip*. The title *Pyeonggeo* means that the first note in the first stanza is in the middle register. Its form is typical for a *gagok*. However, all six of the *Pyeonggeo* in *gyemyeon* mode for females start with "*du ja meori*," which start with two syllables in the first stanza. Therefore, the first three beats at the beginning are omitted and singing starts on the fourth beat. The rhythmic pattern has 16 beats (ten *jeom*) per cycle with basic structure and its tempo is 30 beats per minute.

Hey fishermen who are fishing at the river, do not fry your fish.

Royal officer, his spirit is inside that fish

It could not disappear, no matter how much you steam it.

[a *sijo* referring to the loyalty of Gulwon, an officer of the Cho Dynasty in China (343-278 BC)]

9) *Gyemyeonjo Dugeo*

Derived from *Isudaeyeop*, this song is also called *Joim*, *Jonjajinhanip*, and *Sosakdaeyeop*. The rhythmic pattern has 16 beats (ten *jeom*) per cycle with basic structure and its tempo is 40 beats per minute.

> I get on a boat, on August 16, Imsul year, to Geumreung
>
> Switcher my fish with wine,
>
> But no one to drink it with, since Sodong is now gone.
>
> [a *sijo* commemorating Sosik, a poet in the Song Dynasty, China (1037-1101)]

10) *Pyeongrong*

This is a kind of *nong*, belonging to *sogagok*. The title *Pyeongrong* is named after *Eollong* derived. The rhythmic pattern has 16 beats (ten *jeom*) per cycle with basic structure and its tempo is 50 beats per minute.

> I pray to the seven stars of the Big Dipper
>
> How loathsome is the morning, when I have yet to pour my heart to him
>
> Send those three stars to Venus, tell her to delay.

11) *Urak*

This is a kind of *nak*, belonging to *sogagok*. The title *Urak* is named since it is in *ujo* mode. *Urak* is sung in both male and female voices, female voice begins in a high register while male voice begins in a low register. The rhythmic pattern has 16 beats (ten *jeom*) per cycle with basic structure and its tempo is

Important Intangible Cultural Heritage Holder Kim Yeong-gi, singing *Pyeongrong*

55 beats per minute.

Wind blows like a storm and rain pours.
Could he keep our tryst in this dark storm?
If he should really come, we are meant to be together for good.

12) *Hwangyerak*

This song is found only in a female version. In old sources, *Hwangyerak* did not exist as a separate song and the lyrics were taken from *Urak*. However, as *gagok* became established as arranged songs, when *Urak* in *ujo* mode

Important Intangible Cultural Heritage Holder Jo Sun-ja, singing *Hwangyerak*

shifted to *gyemyeon*, *Hwangyerak* was needed in order to facilitate the transition. Therefore, *Hwangyerak* begins in *ujo* but later changes to *gyemyeonjo*. The rhythmic pattern has 16 beats (ten *jeom*) per cycle with basic structure and its tempo is 55 beats per minute.

> Cowboys, tending cows by the stream
>
> Could you deliver my message, if I gave you all my fish?
>
> We are not sure, we have so little leisure time.

13) *Gyerak*

This is a kind of *nak*, belonging to *sogagok*. Since the mode is *gyemyeon-jo*, it is called *Gyerak*, in contrast to *Urak*. As *gagok* for female voice, this is sung between *Hwangyerak* and *Pyeonsakdaeyeop*. The rhythmic pattern has 16 beats (ten *jeom*) per cycle with basic structure.

> Green hills (will change) on their own, same with the river.
>
> Hills and water shall go as they please and so shall I.
>
> We have come this far, and we shall grow old so naturally.
>
> [a *sijo* using the Korean phrase "*jeollo jeollo*" as rhythmic refrain]

14) *Pyeonsudaeyeop*

Pyeon is a type of *sogagok*. It changes the basic rhythmic pattern of *gagok*, which is 10-*jeom*, 16-beat, to 10-*jeom*, 10-beat pattern, as lyrics becomes more florid. To compensate for the extended lyrics, the rhythm in the third and fifth stanzas is usually extended.

> Peony is the king of all flowers, sunflower is the loyal officer
>
> Lotus is a gentleman, apricot is a man of small character
>
> Chrysanthemum is a monk and cherry blossom, a scholar
>
> Gourd flower is an old man and indian pink, a boy
>
> Hollyhock is a shaman and sweetbrier, a bar lady

Important Intangible Cultural Heritage Holder Kim Yeong-gi, singing *Pyeonsudaeyeop*

> Pear flower is a poet and peach flower a wandering musician.
>
> [a *sijo* which features personification of different kinds of flowers]

15) *Taepyeongga*

This is the last song of the entire *gagok* cycle, and is sung together with a male singer. The melodies of the two parts are different, sometimes a 2nd, 4th, or an octave apart, the combination producing a special sonorous effect.

> We live in such a glorious period,
>
> Like the ancient peaceful days of China.

Important Intangible Cultural Heritage Holder Jo Sun-ja and Teaching Assistant Lee Dong-gyu, singing *Taepyeongga*

Let us enjoy these good days.

[often the final song in a banquet]

The Music-cultural Value of *Gagok*

The Music–cultural Value of *Gagok*

Scholars agree that the *daeyeop*–related songs in the mid–Joseon period, including the *Mandaeyeop*, *Jungdaeyeop*, and *Sakdaeyeop* of *gagok*, originated from *jeonggwajeong samgigok*, which is a kind of indigenous Goryeo music. Among these, *Mandaeyeop*, the slowest of them all, was no longer sung after the late Joseon period, leaving only *Jungdaeyeop* and *Sakdaeyeop*, which then developed and evolved into many different songs and musical genres. With the arrival of the nineteenth century, *Sakdaeyoep* became the mainstream of *gagok*, forming the foundation of many more arrangements and developments. Thus, the current *gagok* ultimately originated from indigenous songs of the Goryeo period.

Moreover, *gagok* bears an important meaning as cultural art, since it uses *sijo*–one of the representative literary forms of the Joseon Dynasty–for its texts. Therefore, by listening to *gagok*, the beauty of *sijo* can be appreciated through music. As *gagok* delivered *sijo* in the form of music, it inspired creativity in the poetry of the period. The latter half of the Joseon period was characterized by a great increase in the number of *sijo*, the majority of which were recorded in song collections. These books were more like anthologies of song lyrics which listed different types of *sijo* poems.

Gagok was one of the most common types of music among the intellectuals of the period and was representative among songs heard and sung among aristocrats in their private gatherings called *pungnyu*. While *Yeongsanhoesang* was the most important instrumental music in the *pungnyu–bang* culture, *gagok* shared its place with *gasa* and *sijo* as the representative vocal music. Although these three were often grouped under the label of *jeongga*, the most important among them was *gagok*. *Gagok* and its singing style became the norm upon which professional singers would base their technique and musical expression. Its relatively slow tempo and sophisticated lyrics, with instrumental accompaniment, were very different from the straightforward and on–the–spot nature of folk songs, nor was it similar to the complicated technicality of *pansori* or *japga*, sung by professional musicians. In that sense, *gagok* reflected the world–view of aristocratic intellectuals of Korean traditional society, and helps to enrich traditional music concerts today.

Gagok was originally the music of amateur musician groups, *pungnyugaek*, and singer–poets, *gagaek*. However, as songs for female singers developed in the nineteenth century and were spread through the activities of court ladies, the music became available to more people. Beginning in the twentieth century, *gagok* was included as one of the ways to cultivate artistry for female entertainers, and came to be enjoyed by the elite class. At the same time, *gagok* was added to the curriculum of the *Aakbuwon Yangseongso*, the training institution for court musicians, becoming more and more a genre for professionals, spread by means of stage performance, recordings, and the mass media.

On the other hand, *gagok* performed at court banquets during the late Joseon period resulted in the vitalization of the female voice, and it came to be used for *changsa*, the singing accompanying court dance, as well. It was arranged for large–scale orchestral works, such as *Jajinhanip*, as well as *saengsobyeongju*, a duet for *saenghwang* and *danso*, and even as solo pieces for *piri*, *daegeum*, or *danso* (such as *Suryongeum*, *Yeomyangchun*, and *Cheongseongjajinhanip*). In its many forms, *gagok* has greatly contributed to enriching the field of vocal performance in Korean traditional music.

Kim Gyeong-bae, Important Intangible Cultural Heritage Holder of *Gagok*

Jo Sun-ja, Important Intangible Cultural Heritage Holder of *Gagok*

Kim Yeong-gi, Important Intangible Cultural Heritage Holder of *Gagok*

| References |

Bangsanhanssigeumbo, 1984, *Hanguk Eumakhak Jaryochongseo* [A Collection of Korean Musicological Sources 14], The National Gukak Center.

Eoeunbo, 1985, *Hanguk Eumakhak Jaryochongseo* [A Collection of Korean Musicological Sources 17], The National Gukak Center.

Gagokwollyu, 1980, *Hanguk Eumakhak Jaryochongseo* [A Collection of Korean Musicological Sources 5], The National Gukak Center.

Geumbosinjeunggaryeong, 1980, *Hanguk Eumakhak Jaryochongseo* [A Collection of Korean Musicological Sources 2], The National Gukak Center.

Geumhapjabo, 1987, *Hanguk Eumakhak Jaryochongseo* [A Collection of Korean Musicological Sources 22], The National Gukak Center.

Hangeumsinbo, 1985, *Hanguk Eumakhak Jaryochongseo* [A Collection of Korean Musicological Sources 8], The National Gukak Center.

Hwigeumgagokbo, 1981, *Hanguk Eumakhak Jaryochongseo* [A Collection of Korean Musicological Sources 7], The National Gukak Center.

Hyeonhakgeumbo, 1999, *Hanguk Eumakhak Jaryochongseo* [A Collection of Korean Musicological Sources 34], The National Gukak Center.

Hyeopryuldaeseong, 1984, *Hanguk Eumakhak Jaryochongseo* [A Collection of Korean Musicological Sources 14], The National Gukak Center.

Jinbon Cheongguyeongeon, 1987, *Sijojayochongseo* [A Collection of Korean Sijo Sources 1], Association of Korean Sijo Literature.

Nangongsinbo, 1984, *Hanguk Eumakhak Jaryochongseo* [A Collection of Korean Musicological Sources 14], The National Gukak Center.

Samjukgeumbo, 1998, *Hanguk Eumakhak Jaryochongseo* [A Collection of Korean Musicological Sources 33], The National Gukak Center.

Unmonggeumbo, 1997, *Hanguk Eumakhak Jaryochongseo* [A Collection of Korean Musicological Sources 16], The National Gukak Center.

Yanggeumsinbo, 1984, *Hanguk Eumakhak Jaryochongseo* [A Collection of Korean Musicological Sources 14], The National Gukak Center.

Yeongeumoeumtongron, 1984, *Hanguk Eumakhak Jaryochongseo* [A Collection of Korean Musicological Sources 14], The National Gukak Center.

Yochanggayorok, 1984, *Hanguk Eumakhak Jaryochongseo* [A Collection of Korean Musicological Sources 16], The National Gukak Center.

Yonsei Daehakgyosojanggeumbo, 1984, *Hanguk Eumakhak Jaryochongseo* [A Collection of Korean Musicological Sources 16], The National Gukak Center.

Yuyeji, 1984, *Hanguk Eumakhak Jaryochongseo* [A Collection of Korean Musicological Sources 15], The National Gukak Center.

Hangukjeongsinmunhwayeonguwon, 1989, *Hanguk Minjokmunhwa Daebaekgwasajeon* [Encyclopedia of Korean Culture], Hangukjeongsinmunhwayeonguwon.

________________________________, 1994. *Jeonghaemuholgi* [Anthology of Court Dance], Hangukjeongsinmunhwayeonguwon.

Hwang Jun-yon, 1980, "Gagokui Hyeongsik [A Form of Gagok]," Hagukeumakyeongu 10, The Korean Musicological Society.

_____________, 1982, "Sakdaeyeopui Hyeongsike gwanhan yeongu [A Study on the form of Gagok], *Hangukeumakhaknonmunjip*, Hanguk Jeongsinmunhwayeonguwon.

_____________, 1982, "Yanggeumsinbo Mandaeyeopui Haedok [An Interpretation of Mandaeyeop `in Yanggeumsinbo]," *Hangukeumakyeongu* 12, The Korean Musicological Society.

_____________, 2001, "Gagok Noraeseonyului Guseongwa Teukjing [The Characteristics and Structure of Male Gagok]," *Hangukeumakyeongu*, The Korean Musicological Society.

Jang Sa-hun, 1966, "Maehwajeomjangdango [A Study of Maehwajeom]," Gukaknongo.

__________, 1976, "Gagokui Yongu [A Study of Gagok]," *Hanguk Eumak Yeongu* 5, The Korean Musicological

Society.

__________, 1983, *Gukaksaron* [A Theory and History of Korean Music], Daegwang Munhwasa.

Jang Sa-hun, Han Man-young, 1975, *Gukakgaeron* [An Introduction to Korean Music], Hanggukgukakhakhoe.

Jo Un-jo, 1976, "Samsudaeyeopgwa Soyong [Samsudaeyeop and Soyong]," MA thesis, Seoul National University.

Kim Hye-jeong, 2008, *Namchang Gagok* [Male Gagok], Minsokwon.

Kim Ki-su, 1979, *Namchang Gagok Baekseon* [A Collection of Male Gagok 100 pieces], Daehandaakwon.

________, 1980, *Yeochang Gagok Yeoeunyeodeolnip* [A Collection of Female Gagok 88 pieces], Daehandaakwon.

Kim Woo-jin, 1984, *Gagok Gyemyeonjoui Nonggwa Nakegwanhayeo* [A Study of Nong and Nak in Gagok], Ph.D. diss, Seoul National University.

Kim Young woon, 2001, "Yeochangagokui Baljeongwajeongedaehan gochal [A Study of Development of Female Gagok]," *Hangukeumakyeongu* 29, The Korean Musicological Society.

______________, 2001, "Yeochangagokui Baljeongwajeongedaehan gochal [A Study of Development of Female Gagok]," *Hangukeumakyeongu* 29, The Korean Musicological Society.

______________, 2001, "Gagokgwa Sijoui Eumaksajeok Jeongae [A Study of Musical Development of Gagok and Sijo]," *Hangukeumaksahabo* 29, The Korean Historico-Musicological Society.

______________, 2004, *Gagok Yeonchanghyeongsikui Jeongaeyangsang Yongu* [A Study of Song-Cycle of Gagok], Ph.D. diss, Sungkyunkwan University.

Lee Hye-ku, 1977, "Hangeumsinboui Ujo Sakdaeyeop [Ujo Sakdaeyeop in Hangeumsinbo], "Dongyangeumak-nonchong.

Seo Han-beom, 2005, *Gagokuibyeonjuyangsanggwa mijeokteukjilegwanhan yeongu* [A Study of Variation of Gagok and Its Aesthetics], Ph.D. diss, Korea University.

Sim Jae-wan, 1972, *Gyobon Yeodaesojeonseo* [A Collection of Sijo], Sejongmunhwasa.

Song Bang-song, 1984, *Hanguk Eumak Tongsa* [A History of Korean Music], Iljogak.